Venice

Front cover: gondolas

Right: carnival mask

The Rialto • The historic heart of Venice's commercial quarter is still famed for its markets *(page 62)*

Collezione Peggy Guggenheim •
One of the best modern art collections in Europe *(page 54)*

Palazzo Ducale •
The splendid former home of the Venetian doges *(page 35)*

Scuola Grande di San Rocco • The interior is decorated with many of Tintoretto's finest paintings *(page 66)*

Murano · This island is world renowned for the fine glass that has been made here for centuries *(page 80)*

La Salute · This iconic landmark stands at the entrance to the Grand Canal *(page 55)*

Basilica di San Marco · The magnificent church at the very heart of Venice *(page 27)*

Bridge of Sighs · Links the Palazzo Ducale with the former jail *(page 38)*

The Accademia · Home to the most pre-eminent collection of Venetian art from the 14th to 18th centuries *(page 50)*

The Grand Canal · The city's spectacular main artery is lined with old palaces *(page 73)*

A PERFECT DAY

9.00am Morning snack

Feast your eyes on the fish, fruit and vegetables of the Rialto markets, where stalls have been in business for over 1,000 years. Watch the barges offloading at the quayside, then browse in local delis for delicious cheeses and pastas.

10.00am Grand Canal

From Rialto take *vaporetto* No. 1 in the San Marco/Lido direction. Glide past the parade of palaces and alight at Accademia.

11.00am Gallery visit

You're now in the *sestiere* of Dorsoduro, a haven for art lovers, home to the Accademia and Guggenheim galleries. Alternatively, just browse around this chic neighbourhood with its little art studios, boutiques and *trattorias*.

1.00pm Lunch with a view

Take your pick from the open-air cafés and restaurants on the Zattere, the panoramic quayside skirting the southern side of the Dorsoduro. For dessert try Gelateria Nico, one of the best ice cream parlours in town.

2.00pm Gentle stroll

Stretch your legs along the Zattere, popping into the Gesuati church to check out the Tiepolo ceiling. Head to the tip of the peninsula where the Punta della Dogana has been transformed into an art gallery, then continue round to the monumental La Salute church.

IN VENICE

4.00pm San Marco tea

Splash out on tea at Caffè Florian in Piazza San Marco, then wander along the Riva degli Schiavoni quayside, taking in the views across to the island of San Giorgio Maggiore.

6.00pm Quiet drink

Leave the crowds behind and explore the streets and squares of the Castello region behind the Riva. Join the locals in a bar for an *ombrà* (glass of wine), Prosecco or *spritz* (a Venetian aperitif), accompanied by *cichetti*, tapas-like snacks.

10.00pm Gondola ride

Pick up a gondola, agree a fee and glide along some of the quieter inland waterways. Alternatively, board the No 1 *vaporetto* for a magical night ride along the Grand Canal – for a fraction of the price of a gondola.

3.00pm Bellini time

Hop on a *vaporetto* to Vallaresso landing stage across the Grand Canal. Pass Harry's Bar (popping in for a bellini if you can't resist) and head north to Salizzada San Moisè and Calle Larga XXII Marzo to browse some of the most fashionable shops in town.

8.00pm Seafood dinner in Castello

For dinner try Alla Rivetta (see page 107) or Da Remigio (see page 108). If you're feeling affluent, Corte Sconta (see pages 107–8) has arguably the best seafood in Venice.

CONTENTS

47

71

42

32

29

43

INTRODUCTION

Venice, the jewel of the Adriatic, is one of a kind. For an unbroken 1,100 years, it was an independent empire and a republic, with a constitution that is studied and admired by students of politics to this day. In the 9th century, while the majority of Europe's cities were hidden behind defensive walls, Venice stood open to the world, protected only by its lagoon. A tantalizing blend of East and West, it was neither totally European nor wholly Italian. Traces of Byzantium and more exotic Asian influences are apparent everywhere.

From a distance the city is a fantasy of sumptuous buildings that seem to float on the surface of the Adriatic. And once you walk its narrow streets *(calli)* or glide along its canals, you cannot fail to be moved by the graceful, exotically romantic architecture that has inspired artists and travellers alike for centuries. While most other great cities have been scarred with main roads and high-rise blocks, Venice remains unsullied by modernity, looking virtually as it did in its heyday.

Geography

Situated at the northwestern end of the Adriatic Sea, Venice lies on an archipelago in a crescent-shaped lagoon 50 km (32 miles) in length. At just 1 metre (3¼ft) above sea-level, Greater Venice stands on 118 flat islets, with its buildings supported by millions of larch poles driven into sediment. Crisscrossing the city is a labyrinth of over

Decorative Venetian mask

Gondoliers on a break

160 canals, spanned by more than 400 bridges. These canals are partly flushed out by the tides that sweep in daily from the Adriatic through three seaways that pierce the ring of sand bars *(lidi)* protecting the lagoon.

The Adriatic

The sea has always been linked with the city's fortunes and, like the swampy, shallow Venetian lagoon, it is loved as if it were part of the city itself. However, with rising sea levels and subsidence caused by falling water tables, Venice has been increasingly swept by flood tides each winter. After many years of debate, construction of the MOSE tidal barrier system began in 2003. The 79 steel flood gates will close the three lagoon inlets when severe floods are forecast. The project is opposed by environmentalists, who argue that the barrier will destroy the delicate ecological balance of the lagoon, to which Venice owes its existence.

Negotiating the City

Any visitor to Venice has to confront its unique geography. To explore the city properly, you have to be prepared to pound the streets – in fact, this is a pleasure in such a car-free environment – and to climb the many bridges that span the canals. This is not a city to visit with excess baggage, as most travellers will at some point have to carry their luggage through sometimes crowded, narrow pedestrian streets and over bridges to their hotels.

When walking becomes tiring, take to the water aboard a *vaporetto* (waterbus). The main *vaporetto* lines ply the Grand Canal, but the system will also take you out to the far corners of the Venetian lagoon from the beaches at the Lido and the brightly painted houses of the island of Burano to the wall-to-wall glass showrooms and factories on Murano and the medieval cathedral set amid the salt meadows on the island of Torcello.

For and Against Tourism

Tourism has become both the lifeblood and the bane of Venice, with 20 million tourists spending at least one day in the city each year. This is nothing new: in his 1912 novella *Death in Venice*, Thomas Mann describes the city as 'half fairy tale, half tourist trap'. Visitors seem to be stung financially at every turn: hotel prices are high by most standards, tourists pay higher fares than residents for use of the *vaporetti*, and restaurants around Piazza San Marco and the other

Water marker

Colourful Burano

main tourist haunts charge grossly inflated prices for food and drink.

And it isn't just the tourists who suffer. In summer the city becomes so packed that it is difficult for anyone to negotiate the narrow streets around Piazza San Marco. The Venetians have become so overwhelmed by the tourist influx, and the city's infrastructure so overburdened by the hordes that there are plans either to limit the number of day-trippers entering the city each day, or to charge admission to visitors who enter without hotel reservations.

Avoiding the Crowds

Yet surcharges and a little extra physical effort are small prices to pay to wander this remarkable place, and if you explore beyond the central area around San Marco, you'll find peaceful neighbourhoods that show the Venice of the Venetians – areas with quirky shops and fairly priced restaurants, cafés and wine bars. This is not to diminish the pleasures of Piazza San Marco, which is undoubtedly one of the world's most beautiful squares, nor its wonderous Basilica and magnificent Palazzo Ducale – even at the height of the season, you can see these sights without being jostled, by simply visiting early or late in the day, when day-trippers are out of the equation.

The Venetians

In its heyday, the city of Venice had 200,000 inhabitants – a figure that fell to 90,000 at the end of the Republic and currently stands at around a mere 60,000. Many apartments have been converted into tourist accommodation and rental prices are well beyond the means of most Venetians. Building restoration costs in Venice are also almost double those of mainland Mestre, from where many former Venetians, especially the younger generation, now commute.

In general, the Venetians are friendly, immensely hospitable and well versed in their city's treasures, although they can often be a little patronising towards anyone 'unfortunate enough' to have been born somewhere else. Their somewhat obscure dialect emphasizes the isolation of Venice. Visitors are often confused by the names of canals or districts spelled varyingly in Italian and Venetian. When asked directions, Venetians are fond of replying, 'Do you want the shortest way, or the beautiful way?' In Venice, however, there is no unattractive way.

The Lions of Venice

Pacific, playful or warlike, lions dominate paintings, sculptures, crests and illuminated manuscripts in Venice; they adorn buildings, bridges, balconies, archways and doorways, with the greatest concentration in the San Marco and Castello districts, closest to the centre of power. Whereas the seated lion represents the majesty of state, the walking lion symbolises Venetian sovereignty over its dominions. The Lion of St Mark bears a traditional greeting of peace and in times of war is depicted with a closed book, as in the arch over the Arsenale gateway. A few lions are shown clutching a drawn sword in one of their paws. The Napoleonic forces were well aware of the symbolism of lions and destroyed many prominent images; as a result, some, such as those on the Gothic gateway to the Palazzo Ducale, are replicas.

A BRIEF HISTORY

It may be hard to believe, but this tiny city was once the centre of the wealthiest, most powerful state in Europe. In its prime, Venice influenced the course of modern history, leaving an incomparable legacy in the shape of the city itself.

Early Venetians

Although the earliest Venetians were fishermen and boatmen skilled at navigating the shallow lagoon's islands, the first major settlers arrived after the Lombards invaded in AD568. The invasion led the coastal dwellers to flee to low-lying off-shore islands in the lagoon, such as Torcello and Malamocco, on the string of *lidi*, or barrier beaches, on the Adriatic.

Venetia, or Venezia, was the name of the entire area at the northern end of the Adriatic under the Roman empire. Venice as we know it developed gradually around a cluster of small islands that remained out of reach of the north Italian Lombard kingdom and were subject only to loose control from the Roman-Byzantine centre at Ravenna, which answered to Constantinople. Around AD697 the lagoon communities were united under a separate military command, set up at Malamocco, with a *dux* (Latin for leader), or doge, in charge. Though the first doges were probably selected by the lagoon dwellers, they still took orders from the Byzantine emperor.

The Lombards were succeeded on the mainland in 774 by Charlemagne's Frankish army, and in 810 his son Pépin was sent to conquer the communities of the lagoon.

Patron saint

When St Mark's relics reached Venice c.829, a chapel (the original St Mark's) was built for them next to the Palazzo Ducale. Mark's winged lion emblem was adopted as the symbol of the city.

Pépin seized the outer island of Malamocco, but the doge and his entourage managed to escape to the safety of the Rivo Alto (High Shore), the future Rialto, where they built a fortress on the site now housing the Palazzo Ducale (Doge's Palace).

The Rise of the Republic

The new city gradually became independent of distant Byzantium, prospering due to tight control of the north Italian river deltas and, later, of the sea itself. Fishing, salt and the lumber and slave trades enriched the city, and rival producers and traders were ruthlessly quashed. From the 9th century, in defiance of the

The arrival of the relics of St Mark, 13th-century mosaic

pope and the Byzantine emperor, the Venetians traded with the Islamic world, selling luxuries from Constantinople at a high profit to the rest of Europe. By this time, Venice was no longer a dependency of the Byzantine Empire, and, to underline this, snatched the body of St Mark from Muslim-controlled Alexandria, in Egypt, c.829. Mark replaced the Byzantine saint, Theodore, as the patron of Venice.

Empire Building

The city's newly founded Arsenale turned out fleets of ever-mightier galleys, enabling Venice to move into the Adriatic, where it warred for decades with its bitter enemy, the

Marco Polo leaving Venice

Dalmatia. In the year 1000, the Republic scored a significant victory and celebrated it with a 'marriage to the sea' ceremony, which is still re-enacted annually *(see page 97)*. Ships flying St Mark's pennant ranged over the Aegean Sea and the eastern Mediterranean, trading, plundering and bringing back spoils to strengthen the state. Venice soon came to be known as the *Serenissima* (Most Serene Republic), or 'Queen of the Seas'.

From the start of the Crusades in 1095, the Venetians sensed rich pickings. Ideally positioned both politically and geographically between Europe and the East, and with little concern for the spiritual aspect of the campaigns, Venice produced and outfitted ships and equipped knights, often at huge profit.

In 1204 crusader armies, under the 90-year-old Doge Enrico Dandalo sacked Constantinople, the greatest repository of the ancient world's treasures. Among the rich pickings were the four bronze horses that adorn the Basilica di San Marco. By now the Republic was a world power, controlling all the major points along the routes to Egypt and the Crimea.

At the end of the 13th century, the Venetians curbed the power of the doges, evolving into a patrician oligarchy. Eventually, the doges became little more than pampered prisoners in their palace, stripped of every vestige of authority; their primary function was to preside over the Republic's pompous festivities, and after 1310 no major change was made in the constitution until the Republic fell in 1797.

Wars and Intrigue

Venice spent much of the 14th century battling with its rival, Genoa, over the slave and grain trades in the Black Sea. They also fought over the route from the Mediterranean north to Bruges and Antwerp, where spices and other wares could be traded for prized Flemish cloth, English wool and tin. In 1379, during the fourth and final Genoese War, Venice came closer to defeat than at any time in its history: the Genoese fleet, aided by Hungarian and Paduan troops, captured and sank Venetian ships in home waters. When the key port of Chioggia, south of Venice, was taken, the *Serenissima* seemed lost. The Venetians retook the port, however, and in 1380 Genoa surrendered, forever finished as a major maritime force.

The 14th century was also a time for domestic difficulties. In 1310 a group of disgruntled aristocrats under Baiamonte Tiepolo tried to seize power and kill the doge, but their revolt was quickly crushed. Worse was to come: between 1347 and 1349 almost half of the city's population of 120,000 was wiped out by the Black Death. A further 20,000 Venetians died in another epidemic in 1382, and over the next three centuries the city was almost never free of plague.

Marco Polo

Venice's most famous citizen opened the eyes of 13th-century Europe to the irresistibly exotic mysteries of Asia. While recent scholarship has thrown some doubt on the authenticity of his story, Marco Polo relates how, for some 20 years, he served the Mongol emperor Kublai Khan and was the first Westerner permitted to travel about freely in China. When he came back from China, legend has it that nobody recognized him or believed his tales – until he slit the seams of his clothes and precious jewels fell out.

Doge Loredan by Bellini

The Republic began to focus attention on its land boundary. As an expanding manufacturing city in the 15th century, it needed food, wood and metal from the nearest possible sources. However, its push along the northern Italian rivers and across the plain of Lombardy soon met with opposition, and the conflicts known as the Lombard Wars began in 1425. The Republic defended its new territory so tenaciously that Milan, Florence and Naples formed an anti-Venice coalition, worried that Venice might take over the entire Italian peninsula.

New Threats in a Golden Age

With the dying Byzantine Empire no longer able to buffer Venice against threats from the east, a new rival arose in the shape of the Ottoman Empire. Initially, the young sultan, Mohammed the Conqueror, was not taken seriously, and inadequate forces were sent by the Venetians to protect Constantinople. In 1453 the city fell to the Turks, who played havoc with Venetian trade routes and won a key naval battle at Negroponte in the northern Aegean in 1470. Although Venice was still the leading Mediterranean maritime power, these defeats marked the beginning of a downhill slide.

While its fortunes beyond the lagoon waned, Venetian civilisation reached new heights. No building in the Western world was more sumptuous than the Palazzo Ducale; no church had as many treasures as San Marco. And as artists such as Bellini, Giorgione, Carpaccio, Tintoretto, Veronese and Titian flourished, Andrea Palladio's revolutionary concepts began to shape the future of architecture. Venice was also home to the most complex economy and the richest culture in all Europe.

Yet the threats to the Republic continued to accumulate. In 1498 Vasco da Gama of Portugal undertook his epic voyage around the Cape of Good Hope to India, opening up new trade routes and putting an end to Venice's spice-trade monopoly. During the same period of prodigious exploration, Christopher Columbus's landfalls on the other side of the Atlantic proved momentous for the Venetian Republic. The axis of power in Europe gradually moved to countries on the Atlantic coast. As trade with the New World mushroomed, the Oriental trade that had long ensured Venetian prosperity fell into decline.

Decline and Decadence

After the French invasion of Italy in 1494, Venice sought to further encroach on the latter. However, this international brinkmanship so incensed the rest of Europe that, in 1508, under the auspices of Pope Julius II and the king of Spain, a pan-European organisation, known as the League of Cambrai, was formed with the aim of destroying the Republic. City after city defected, as the Republic's 20,000-strong mercenary army fell apart. For a while things seemed desperate, but the League itself fell apart through internal struggles, and Venice managed to regain nearly all its territories. However, seven years of war cost the Venetians dearly, putting a stop to their ambitions in Italy. Furthermore, with Charles V's empire steadily accumulating Italian ground, considerable Venetian diplomacy was needed for the city to preserve its independence.

Around the eastern and southern Mediterranean, the Ottomans surged on, and the Battle of Lepanto, in 1571, finally

View of the Ducal Palace in Venice (c.1755) by Canaletto

turned the Turkish tide. The fleet of the Holy League was spearheaded by Venice, but the allies, by now suspicious of Venice, ensured that the city did not profit from this victory; instead of continuing the offensive east, they signed away the Venetian stronghold of Cyprus as part of the peace treaty.

From 1575 to 1577 plague raged again, and the population fell from 150,000 to 100,000. Despite this, and the Republic's diminishing political powers, Venice prospered through the 16th and 17th centuries, aided by the skills and contacts of Jewish refugees from the Italian peninsula and Spain. Music flourished, with Claudio Monteverdi in the 17th century and Antonio Vivaldi in the 18th. Venice's art tradition continued with Tiepolo and Canaletto, and the playwright Carlo Goldoni's new adaptations of *commedia dell'arte* broke exciting ground. If the city was a fading world power, it fast warmed to its new role as the playground of Europe, staging extravagant carnival balls and becoming notorious for gambling.

The End of the Republic

By the end of the 18th century the Venetians knew that Napoleon was on the war path but were simply too weak to stop him. He entered the city, demanding that the government turn its power over to a democratic council under French military protection. In 1797 the last doge, Ludovico Manin, abdicated, the Great Council voted to dissolve itself, and the *Serenissima* was no more. Napoleon's troops looted and destroyed the Arsenale, but they stayed in Venice for only five months, until their emperor was forced to relinquish it to Austrian control. However, in 1805, Napoleon returned, having defeated the Austrians at Austerlitz, and he made the city part of his short-lived Kingdom of Italy.

After Waterloo, the Austrians again occupied Venice, and stayed for more than 50 years, until 1866. Although the Austrians were despised by the Venetians, they did restore to the city most of the artistic booty taken by Napoleon. In 1846 they linked Venice to the mainland for the first time, erecting an unsightly railway bridge. In 1848, the Venetians rose up under revolutionary leader Daniele Manin and ousted the Austrian garrison; however, their provisional republic fell the following year. In 1866, after Austria's defeat by Prussia, the Venetians voted overwhelmingly to join the new Kingdom of Italy.

The City Today

Although Venice remained virtually untouched by the two world wars, it was not without its troubles in the 20th century. The construction of a large commercial

Casa or palazzo?

Until the late 17th century the Palazzo Ducale was the only building in Venice that was allowed to be called a *palazzo*. Other splendid mansions were called simply Casa (house), shortened to Ca'. Many families did not bother to rename their houses *palazzi* once it was permitted, hence Ca' d'Oro, Ca' da Mosto and so on.

harbour and oil refinery at Porto Marghera in the 1920s and 1930s caused significant pollution problems. By tapping the region's water table, it created both flooding and sinking conditions and provoked a harmful build-up of algae. Following disastrous floods in November 1966, when the city was flooded for 13 hours up to a depth of nearly 2m (over 6ft), local and international organisations were set up to restore buildings and works of art in the city and to bring Venice's plight to world attention. In 1992 the Italian government released funds for the MOSE project, a system of huge mobile flood protection barriers to be constructed at the Porto di Lido, Porto di Malamocco and Porto di Chioggia. After years of political debate the project was finally inaugurated in 2003, but cuts in government funding have caused the projected completion date to slip from 2010 to 2014.

Paradoxically, the city's biggest problem nowadays is also its most lucrative trade – tourism. At peak season, a daily influx of 55,000 tourists takes its toll on the city's fragile infrastructure and threatens to destroy the very sights they have come to admire. Meanwhile, the city's mayor, Massimo Cacciari, has been criticised for allowing vast advertising hoardings in Piazza San Marco.

Flooding in Piazza San Marco

Cacciari claims the revenue is crucial for the upkeep of the city, but his critics argue he is destroying the city in order to save it. The protection of Venice, whether by flood gates, reversing the exodus of the local population, controlling the number of visitors or doing deals with giant multinationals, will always be the city's most contentious issue.

Historical Landmarks

6th century AD Refugees fleeing barbarians settle in the lagoon.

696 Election of Paoluccio Anafesto as the first doge.

828 The body of St Mark, stolen from Alexandria, is smuggled to Venice.

991–1008 Doge Pietro Orseolo II reigns. Commercial advantages are gained from Byzantium, and a sea battle is won against Dalmatia.

1104 The Arsenale is founded.

1202–4 Venice diverts the Fourth Crusade and sacks Constantinople.

1347–9 Nearly half the city's population wiped out by the Black Death.

1380 War with Genoa ends in a Venetian victory at Chioggia.

1405 Venice takes Verona from Milan.

1423 Election of Doge Francesco Foscari begins Venetian expansion to Bergamo and Brescia and on to parts of Cremona.

1453 The Turks take Constantinople, heralding the expansion of the Ottoman Empire in Europe.

1498 Vasco da Gama reaches the East Indies, marking the beginning of the end for Venice's spice monopoly.

1508 The League of Cambrai against Venice results in territorial losses.

1571 Resounding victory against the Turks at Lepanto.

1797 Napoleonic troops enter Venice, and the Republic comes to an end.

1815 The Treaty of Vienna places the Veneto under Austrian control.

1848 Under Daniele Manin, Venice rebels against Austria.

1866 Venice becomes part of unified Italy.

1914–18 World War I. More than 600 bombs are dropped on Venice.

1920s/1930s Commercial harbour and oil refinery built at Marghera.

1966 Disastrous flooding leads to the launch of an international appeal.

1979 The Venice Carnival is revived.

1994 Approval of MOSE, a mobile dam designed to prevent flooding.

1996 Most severe floods for 30 years; fire at La Fenice opera house.

2002 The euro replaces the Italian lira as the country's unit of currency.

2008 The Calatrava Bridge is erected over the Grand Canal. In December record high tides flood the city.

2009 The Punta della Dogana Contemporary Art Centre opens.

WHERE TO GO

The incomparable *palazzi*, canals and lagoons of Venice present something of a fantasy world, even to the most seasoned of travellers. At times of winter floods, Carnival shenanigans or the peak of summer, when tourists descend en masse, the myth may seem at risk of turning into a nightmare; yet even at these hectic times you can still take refuge in a café once frequented by Casanova or a quiet alley that looks just as it did 400 years ago.

Venice is traditionally divided into six *sestieri* (districts). The obvious place to start is San Marco with its famous church and piazza. To the east is Castello, home to several major churches and the Arsenale. South and west of San Marco, on the other side of the Grand Canal, is Dorsoduro with its art galleries and university, and north of there, inside the northern bend of the Grand Canal, are the adjoining districts of San Polo and Santa Croce. Finally, further north, with the railway station and former Jewish Ghetto, is Cannaregio.

A great bonus in Venice is the absence of cars – stand on a little humpbacked bridge, far from the Grand Canal, and all you'll hear is the water lapping against the mossy walls, or the swish of a gondola that appears out of nowhere. Despite its watery character, most of the city is best explored on foot, with the occasional boat trip thrown in for a new perspective or to reach the far corners of the lagoon.

The Rialto Bridge

When to visit

Visit Venice in May or October if you can – the crowds at Easter and from June to September can be frustrating. Christmas in Venice has also become quite fashionable; though the city can be dank and cold in winter, it takes on a rather mystical beauty at this time.

Basilica di San Marco

SAN MARCO

The first area in Venice that most visitors head for is San
Marco, home to several of the city's main landmarks, notably
the Piazza and Basilica of San Marco.

Piazza San Marco

The main square in Venice, **Piazza San Marco**, is a hectic
spot, bustling with tour groups and sightseers. The square
was originally the site of a monastery garden with a canal
running through it, but since its transformation in the 12th
and 13th centuries it has been the religious and political centre of the city. The Piazza has always pulled in the crowds –
at the peak of the Republic's powers, some of the world's
most spectacular processions, such as the one depicted in
Gentile Bellini's celebrated painting at the Accademia *(see
page 53)*, were staged here. Victorious commanders return-

ing home from the Genoese or Turkish wars were fêted in front of the Basilica with grand parades, while vendors on the square sold sweets and snacks, much as they do today. And under the arcades, Venetians and tourists have promenaded and been enchanted by elegant shops for centuries.

Yet despite all its pomp and circumstance and hustle and bustle, the Piazza remains a very civilised place. Dubbed by Napoleon the 'finest drawing room in Europe', it is elegantly proportioned, with colonnades on three sides, and fringed with exquisite monuments (most dating from the 16th and 17th centuries). Interestingly, the 'square' is actually a trapezoid, with uneven pavements sloping slightly downwards towards the Basilica. Its trachyte (volcanic rock) paving strips are more than 250 years old and lie over five or six earlier layers of tiles from the mid-13th century.

Basilica di San Marco

Blending Eastern and Western elements, the **Basilica di San Marco** (St Mark's Basilica; Mon–Sat, Apr–Oct 9.45am–5pm, Nov–Mar until 4pm, Sun and hols 2–5pm, Nov–Mar until 4pm; www.basilicasanmarco.it; leave bags in the Ateneo San Basso, Calle San Basso 315/A) is an exquisite, sumptuous shrine, encapsulating the old Republic's vision of itself as the successor to Constantinople. Despite the sloping irregular floors, an eclectic mix of styles both inside and out, the five low domes of totally unequal proportions and some 500 non-matching columns, San Marco still manages to convey a sense of grandeur as well as a jewel-like delicacy.

The church was originally built in AD830 as a chapel for the doges and as a rest-

Jump the queue

To avoid the long queues for the Basilica di San Marco reserve a free ticket in advance at www.alata.it. Take it to the special entrance for those with bookings.

Mosaic in the narthex

ing place for the remains of St Mark, which had just been stolen from Alexandria by two Venetian adventurers *(see page 15)*. According to legend, they hid the body in a consignment of salted pork; Muslim customs officials, forbidden by their religion from eating or coming in contact with pork, did not do a thorough search and let the relics slip through their fingers. Not only were the body and many of the adornments in the Basilica stolen from the East but most of the church's columns were also brought back as booty from forays into the Levant. The Basilica became the Republic's shrine as well as the coronation place of its doges. However, the original, largely wooden church burned down in 976, and the Basilica we see today was constructed between 1063 and 1094; its exterior was then lavishly decorated with marble and ornamentation over the next three centuries.

The Narthex

The small porch at the entrance to the cathedral (the narthex) gives visitors their first sight of the fabulous **mosaics** that are a predominant feature of the church's interior. Described by the poet W.B. Yeats as 'God's holy fire', they are said to cover a total area of around 0.5 hectares (1 acre). The narthex mosaics date from the 13th century and are among the most spectacular in the whole Basilica; they depict such Old Testament events as the Creation and the story of Noah's ark. The mosaics are at their best from 11.30am–12.30pm daily when the cathedral is illuminated.

Museo Marciano

The staircase immediately to the right of the main entrance leads to a small museum, the **Museo Marciano** (charge), housing some of the San Marco's finest treasures. The star attraction is the world's only surviving ancient *quadriga* (four horses abreast), known as the **Cavalli di San Marco** (The Horses of St Mark) and cast around AD200, either in Rome or Greece. At one time, the horses were believed to have crowned Trajan's Arch in Rome, but they were later moved to the imperial hippodrome in Constantinople, where Doge Dandolo claimed them as spoils of war in 1204, bringing them back to Venice. After guarding the shipyard of the Venetian Arsenale for a while, the *quadriga* was moved to

The Cavalli di San Marco, stolen from Constantinople

the front of the cathedral, becoming almost as symbolic of the city as St Mark's trademark lion.

In 1378 the rival republic of Genoa boasted that it would 'bridle those unbridled horses', but it never succeeded. Napoleon managed to corral them, however, taking them to Paris to stand on the Place du Carrousel adjacent to the Louvre for 13 years. When Venice fell under Austrian rule, the Austrians restored the horses to San Marco, where they remained until World War I, when the Italian government moved them to Rome. During World War II they were moved again, this time into the nearby countryside. After the war, they were returned to the Basilica, although the ones on display at the front of the cathedral are only replicas – the original *quadriga* was moved inside to protect it against corrosion from air pollution. The Venetians have vowed that the horses will never be allowed to leave their city again.

Detail of the Pala d'Oro

The galleries in which the museums are situated provide good views of the interior; while outside on the Loggia dei Cavalli you can look down on Piazza San Marco and the adjacent piazzetta.

> **Dress code**
>
> Visitors in short shorts or skirts will not be allowed entry to Venice's churches, especially the Basilica di San Marco. Shoulders and backs must also be covered.

The Treasury and High Altar

Located just off the baptistery on the Basilica's right-hand side is the **Tesoro** (Treasury; charge), where you can see further riches looted from Constantinople at the time of the Fourth Crusade (1204). Close by is the **Altare Maggiore** (High Altar), which bears a *ciborium* (canopy) mounted on four alabaster columns dating from the seventh or eighth century; sculpted scenes from the lives of Christ and the Virgin Mary adorn the altar. In the illuminated grating is a sarcophagus containing the relics of St Mark.

The Pala d'Oro

Behind the altar is one of Christendom's greatest treasures, the **Pala d'Oro** (charge), a gold, bejewelled altar screen featuring dozens of scenes from the *Bible*. Originally crafted in the 12th century, the screen was embellished and enlarged on the doges' orders until it reached its present stage in the mid-14th century. Its exquisitely wrought golden frame holds the Venetian equivalent of the Crown Jewels: 1,300 pearls, 400 garnets, 300 sapphires, 300 emeralds, 90 amethysts, 75 balas-rubies, 15 rubies, four topazes and two cameos.

The only drawback to the fabulous splendour of the Pala d'Oro is that it attracts hordes of sightseers. The best way to try and beat the crowds is to visit either early in the morning, before day-trippers and tour groups have arrived, or late in the afternoon, after they have left.

The Campanile

Campanile di San Marco

For breathtaking views of Piazza San Marco and the city, ascend the **Campanile di San Marco** (St Mark's Belltower; daily, Apr–June and Oct 9.30am–7pm, July–Sept 9am–9pm, Nov–Mar 9.30am–3.45pm; charge), at 100m (335ft) Venice's tallest building, which over the years has served as a light-house, gun turret and belfry. Within less than a minute a lift takes you to the top, where the exotic domes of the Basilica, the splendid wedge-shaped tip of the Dorsoduro (marking the start of the Grand Canal), the island church of San Giorgio Maggiore and the terracotta-coloured tiles of the an-cient city roofscape are spread beneath your feet. The scene looks much the same now as it did over 200 years ago when the German writer J.W. von Goethe came here for his first view of the sea. It may well even look the same as four cen-turies ago when, according to local lore, Galileo brought the doge up here to show off his new telescope. Intriguingly, not a single canal can be seen from the Campanile.

However, this most potent symbol of the city is not the original tower, which collapsed into the Piazza on 14 July 1902. Fortunately, the old building creaked and groaned so much in advance that everyone knew what was coming – numerous belltowers in Venice have fallen down over the centuries, so the locals were used to it and knew to keep their distance; the eventual collapse caused no injury. Contrary to the 'evidence' supplied on cleverly faked postcards on sale throughout the city, the moment was not caught on film.

The city council quickly decided to rebuild the bell tower 'as it was, where it was', and precisely 1,000 years after the erection of the original Campanile, on 25 April 1912 a new, lighter version was inaugurated. However, like many Venetian belltowers, this one is already starting to lean.

Piazzetta dei Leoncini

The small square situated to the left as you face the Basilica is known as the **Piazzetta dei Leoncini**, after the two marble lions that have been here since 1722. On the side of the Basilica facing the Piazzetta is the tomb of Daniele Manin, the leader of Venice's revolt against Austria and the subsequent, short-lived Venetian Republic of 1848–9. A descendent of a family from the Venetian Ghetto, the heroic Manin was reinterred in this site of unequalled honour after the end of the Austrian Occupation in 1866, along with his wife and children – none of the doges was granted such a splendid resting place.

Torre dell'Orologio

The Campanile is not the Piazza's only notable belltower – the graceful **Torre dell'Orologio** (Clock Tower; tours by appointment only, in English Mon–Wed at 10am and 11am, Thur–Sun at 1pm, 2pm and 3pm, tel: 041-520 9070, www.museicivicivenezani.it; charge), features a splendid **zodiacal clock** that shows the time in both Arabic and Roman numerals and has been ticking for over 500 years. On Epiphany in January and through Ascension week in May three bright-eyed Magi and a trumpeting angel swing out from the face of the clock tower on the stroke of every hour and, stiffly bowing, ceremoniously rotate around a gilded Madonna.

At the top of the tower, two scantily clad North African bronze figures use hammers to strike a bell. According to Venetian legend, stroking the figures' exposed nether regions confers sexual potency for a year. Venetians also claim that a workman was knocked off the top of the tower in the 19th century by one of the hammers – perhaps a kind of revenge for the impertinence that the statues have to endure.

Procuratie Vecchie and Nuove

Adjacent to the Torre dell'Orologio is the colonnaded **Procuratie Vecchie**, built in the 16th century as a home for the Procurators of San Marco (state officers charged with the administration of the *sestieri*, or Venetian districts). Below it is one of Venice's two most famous cafés, the Caffè Quadri, favoured haunt of the Austrians during their occupation of the city in the 19th century.

The church of San Geminiano once stood at the far end of the Piazza opposite the Basilica, but in 1807 Napoleon ordered it to be demolished in order to make way for a wing joining the two sides of the square. On the facade of this wing, known as the **Ala Napoleonica** (Napoleon's Wing), there are several statues of Roman emperors and a central niche originally intended for a statue of Napoleon himself but pointedly left empty.

Opposite the Procuratie Vecchie is the **Procuratie Nuove**, built between 1582 and 1640 as a new home for the Procurators, and later occupied by Napoleon as a royal palace. The Museo Correr *(see page 40)* now occupies most of the upper floors of this building and the adjacent Ala Napoleonica. Below the Procuratie Nuove, on the side of the square facing Caffè Quadri, is the Piazza's other famous café, Florian. Founded in 1720, but with a mid-19th-century interior, it may be the oldest continuously operating café in the world.

Palace facade

Palazzo Ducale

For nine centuries the magnificent **Palazzo Ducale** (Doge's ◀ ❸ Palace; daily, Apr–Oct 9am–7pm, Nov–Mar 9am–5pm, last entrance one hour before closing time; www.museicivici veneziani.it; charge) was the seat of the Republic, serving as a council chamber, law court and prison, as well as the residence of most of Venice's doges. The Palazzo was first built in fortress-like Byzantine style in the 9th century and partially replaced 500 years later by a Gothic structure. The architects of this massive structure, with peach-and-white patterning in its brick facade, achieved an incredible delicacy by balancing the bulk of the building above two floors of Gothic arcades. The ravages inflicted by three devastating fires have necessitated some extensive reconstruction work over the centuries.

The palace's 15th-century ceremonial entrance, the **Porta della Carta** (Paper Gate), is a masterpiece of late Gothic stonework. Its name may derive from the fact that the doge's decrees were affixed here, or from the professional scribes who set up nearby. On the left, note the four curious dark brown figures of the Tetrarchs (also known as the 'Four Moors'), variously said to represent the Roman emperor Diocletian and associates, or four Saracen robbers who tried to loot the Basilica's Treasury *(see page 31)* through the wall behind them.

Visits start at the Porta del Frumento on the lagoon side of the palace. The **Museo dell' Opera** by the entrance houses some of the original carved capitals from the palazzo's loggias. Inside the courtyard is the impressive ceremonial stairway, the **Scala dei Giganti**, named after Sansovino's colossal statues of Neptune and Mars (symbolising, respectively, Venetian sea and land powers). Visitors use the only slightly less grandiose **Scala d'Oro** (Golden Staircase), which was built during the 16th century to designs by Jacopo Sansovino.

The Interior

The main tour of the palace begins in the state rooms, in which the business of the Republic was once conducted. This part of the complex is home to some of the finest paintings in the ducal collection. On the walls in front of and behind you as you enter the **Anticollegio** are four allegories by Tintoretto, combining images of pagan gods and the four seasons to suggest that Venice is favoured at all times. Jacob Bassano's *Jacob Returning to Canaan* is on the wall opposite the windows, on your right. To the left of it is Veronese's masterpiece, *The Rape of Europa*.

The gilded ceiling in the Anticollegio

The impressive Sala del Maggior Consiglio

Proceed on to the **Sala del Collegio**, where the doges received ambassadors. Next is the **Sala del Senato** where the Venetian ruling council (made up of the doge, his advisors, members of the judiciary and senators) formulated policy.

The next room is the **Sala del Consiglio dei Dieci**, the meeting room of the Council of Ten. The Ten (who actually numbered up to 17) were a high-ranking group that met on matters of state security and acquired a reputation similar to that of the secret police. A letter-box in the form of a lion's mouth, for the use of citizens who wished to inform the Ten of anything untoward, can be seen in the next room.

On the public route, the palace's somewhat menacing aura is confirmed by a splendid private armoury, in which some extremely gruesome weapons are displayed.

The route then leads down to the first-floor state rooms. The most resplendent of all, is the **Sala del Maggior Consiglio** (Great Council Chamber), a vast hall where Venetian citizens assembled to elect doges and debate state policies in the early days of the Republic. Later, only the nobles convened here. The hall was built to hold an assembly of up to 1,700, but by the mid-16th century this figure had increased to around 2,500. Covering the whole of one end wall is Tintoretto's *Paradiso*, based on Dante's masterpiece, and undertaken by the artist (with the assistance of his son) while he was in his seventies. At 7m by 22m (23ft by 72ft), it is the largest old master oil painting in the world, containing some 350 human figures. Adorning the ceiling is Veronese's *Apotheosis of Venice*, which captures the ideal civic conception of Venice as serene, prosperous, elegant and self-assured. Portraits of 76 doges (several of which are little more than artistic guesswork) line the cornice beneath the ceiling. Conspicuously absent is the 14th-century doge, Marin Falier – a black veil marks his intended place of honour, and a notice tells us that he was beheaded for treason in 1355.

From here the tour takes you to the criminal courts and the Prigioni Nuove (New Prisons), which are reached by the legendary **Bridge of Sighs** (Ponte dei Sospiri). The baroque stone bridge, built in 1614, was given its evocative name by Lord

Secret Tours of the Palace

The Itinerari Segreti is a fascinating guided tour (in English daily at 9.55am, 10.45am and 11.35am), which gives access to secret parts of the Doge's Palace that are normally off limits to visitors. The tour takes around 1 hour 15 minutes and includes the torture chamber (in reality far less gruesome than it sounds) and the cell from which Casanova, one of Venice's most notorious citizens, escaped in 1775. The tour ticket also gives access to the rest of the palace. Advance bookings can be made until 2 days before the visit (tel: 041-271 5911, www.museiciviciveneziani. it) or, if still available, on the day by asking at the information desk.

Byron who wrote: 'I stood in Venice on the Bridge of Sighs, a palace and a prison on each hand'. The idea that condemned prisoners sighed at their last glance of Venice when crossing the bridge derives more from romantic fiction than hard fact, since by the time the bridge was built only petty criminals would have made this journey. The bridge has two parallel passageways, each leading to different court and interrogation rooms. On the other side are the small, dark cells where prisoners were kept, which are relatively civilised by medieval standards.

The Bridge of Sighs

Piazzetta San Marco

If Piazza San Marco is the drawing room of Venice, the smaller **Piazzetta San Marco** is its vestibule. The two soaring granite columns dominating the piazzetta were stolen from the East and hoisted upright here in 1172. They haven't moved since, although a third column apparently fell into the sea.

On top of one of the columns is Venice's original patron saint, St Theodore; on the other stands what must be the strangest looking of the city's many stone lions – not really a lion at all but a *chimera*, a mythical hybrid beast (you can see it most clearly from the balcony of the Palazzo Ducale). Even though its exact origin is unknown, it is thought to be of Eastern provenance and may be up to 2,200 years old.

Gran Caffè Chioggia on Piazzetta San Marco

Nowadays the area bustles with tourists, but between the 15th and mid-18th centuries it was a place of execution. One of the more creative punishments involved torturing the prisoner, burning them on a raft, dragging them through the streets and finally putting them to death between the columns.

Museo Correr and Museo Archeologico

There are two museums on Piazza San Marco, both of which are usually not too crowded. The **Museo Correr** (daily Apr–Oct 10am–7pm, Nov–Mar 10am–5pm, last entrance one hour before closing time; www.museicivicivceneziani.it; charge) occupies some 70 rooms of the Ala Napoleonica and Procuratie Nuove. It is home to the city museum and contains artefacts from virtually every aspect of Venice's history. It houses a fine collection of 14th- to 16th-century Venetian paintings, including a room of works by Jacopo Bellini and his sons, Giovanni and Gentile. Vittorie Carpaccio's *Two Venetian Noblewomen,* traditionally and erroneously known as *The Courtesans*, is also displayed here. Other highlights include sculpture by Canova, wonderful old globes and incredible stilt-like platform shoes worn by 15th-century Venetian courtesans. Also within the Correr is the **Museo del Risorgimento**, which illustrates the history of Venice from the 19th century onwards.

The **Museo Archeologico** (Archaeological Museum; daily 8.15am–7.15pm), is accessed through Museo Correr. It occupies part of the lavish 16th-century building opposite the Palazzo Ducale on Piazzetta San Marco. The core collection here consists of Greek and Roman sculpture bequeathed by Cardinal Grimani in 1523, a gift that influenced generations of Venetian artists who came to study here. Among the Roman busts, medals, coins, cameos and portraits are Greek originals and Roman copies, including a 5th-century Hellenistic *Persephone*.

Biblioteca Marciana

In the other part of the building opposite the Palazzo Ducale, and likewise accessed through Museo Correr, is the **Biblioteca Nazionale Marciana** (National Library of St Mark; charge, free guided tours Sun–Thur at 10am, noon and 2pm, tel: 041-240 7223), also known as the Libreria Sansoviniana after its architect Jacopo Sansovino. The magnificent main hall of the original library is decorated with paintings by Veronese, Tintoretto and other leading artists of the time.

Just a few yards behind the library are the **Giardinetti Reali** (Royal Gardens). There are also tourist information offices *(see pages 127–8)* in the neighbouring Venice Pavilion and at the southwest exit of Piazza San Marco.

Museum pass

Keen sightseers can cut costs by purchasing a San Marco Museum Plus Pass at www.museiciviciveneziani.it. This covers the Doge's Palace, Museo Correr, Museo Archeologico and Biblioteca Marciana.

The perfectly proportioned Scala del Bovolo

Also in San Marco

If you have more time to explore San Marco *sestiere*, there is an intriguing tower, an opera house and a Gothic church within a few minutes' walk of Piazza San Marco.

Hidden in a maze of alleys between Calle Vida and Calle Contarini, close to Campo Manin, is **Palazzo Contarini del Bovolo** (Apr–Oct daily 10am–6pm, Nov–Mar Sat–Sun 10am–4pm, but closed for restoration until at least 2011; charge), a late-Gothic palace renowned for its romantic arcaded staircase, the **Scala del Bovolo**. *Bovolo* means 'snail-shell' in Venetian dialect and fittingly describes this graceful spiral staircase, which is linked to loggias of brick and smooth white stone. Although the palace is currently closed you don't need access to admire the beautiful stairway.

La Fenice (open for 45-minute tours from 10am–6pm; tel: 041-2424; charge), the city's main opera house, is located on Campo San Fantin, west of Piazza San Marco. One of the world's loveliest opera auditoriums, it was almost completely destroyed by fire in 1838, but rose again 'like a phoenix' *(fenice)*, rebuilt almost exactly. After fire struck again in 1996, the theatre has once again been restored to its former glory and the latest fire precautions installed.

The Gothic **Santo Stefano** church (Mon–Sat 10am–5pm; charge), located on Campo Santo Stefano, west of the opera house, is a large, airy structure decorated with rich ornamentation and works by Tintoretto.

CASTELLO

The eastern region of Venice, Castello is the largest of the city's *sestieri*. The name derives from a former 8th century castle built on the island of San Pietro in the east. Castello is home to the Arsenale, where the great Venetian galleys were built, the fine Gothic church of Santi Giovanni e Paolo and the Scuola di San Giorgio degli Schiavoni with its exquisite frieze of paintings by Carpaccio.

Along the Waterfront

There are few more stately waterfronts in the world than that of Venice's splendid *riva* (quay), which curves gently away from San Marco towards the *sestiere* of Castello. The first section, the **Riva degli Schiavoni** (Quay of the Slavs), begins in front of the Palazzo Ducale *(see page 35)*. The bustling quay

Gondolas moored along the quay

Bellini's *Madonna and Child* in the church of San Zaccaria

takes its name from the Dalmatian merchants who used to tie up their boats here – vessels laden with wares from the East. This is still a place of trade, though less exotic than in its heyday, with souvenir stalls and ice-cream and refreshment stands lining the banks. Boats still moor here, too: *vaporetti* (waterbuses) at the busy station of San Zaccaria and fleets of gondolas waiting to tempt tourists.

After the Palazzo Ducale, the next sight you'll see (with your back to the waterfront) is the Bridge of Sighs *(see pages 38–9)*. A little further on is the red **Palazzo Dandolo**, now the legendary **Hotel Danieli**, with a lavish neo-Gothic lobby that's worth a look. When Proust stayed here, he declared, 'When I went to Venice I found that my dream had become – incredibly but quite simply – my address'. The Danieli was also the scene of an unhappy love affair between the writers George Sand and Alfred de Musset in 1883.

A little further on, after the colonnaded Ponte del Vin, the second turning to the left leads away from the waterfront to a quiet *campo* overlooked by the splendid 16th-century church of **San Zaccaria** (daily 10am–noon, 4–6pm). Supposedly the last resting place of Zaccharias (the father of John the Baptist), whose body lies in the right aisle, this Gothic-Renaissance masterpiece features Giovanni Bellini's celebrated *Madonna and Child*. The side chapels have splendid glowing altarpieces, and the eerie, permanently flooded 8th-century crypt, where several early doges rest in watery graves, is one of the most atmospheric spots in the city.

Back on the waterfront, continue eastwards for the church of **La Pietà** (daily 9.30am–noon), a handsome building with a fine ceiling painting by Giambattista Tiepolo. It is known as 'Vivaldi's church', after Antonio Vivaldi who was concert-master here from 1705 to 1740.

Carry on past the statue of King Vittorio Emanuele II and you'll notice the crowds starting to thin out. By the time you reach the Arsenale *vaporetto* stop, just a short distance from the Palazzo Ducale, the crowds will probably have dispersed completely, even in high season.

The Arsenale
For 700 years, before Napoleon's invasion in the late 18th century, the Republic's galleys and galleons were built at the **Arsenale** (closed to the public), once the greatest shipyard in the world. Dante visited it, and used the images of its work-

Italian naval officers outside the Arsenale

ers toiling amid cauldrons of boiling pitch as the inspiration for his *Inferno*. *Arsenale*, originally from the Arabic for 'house of industry', is one of those Venetian coinages that have passed into universal usage. The yard also originated the concept of the assembly line. Output was prodigious.

One of the yard's proudest achievements came in 1574, while Henri III of France was visiting Venice. In the time it took for the French king to get through his state banquet at the Palazzo Ducale, the workers at the Arsenale had constructed a fully equipped galley from scratch, ready for the king's inspection.

Today, there's little to remind visitors of those heady days. Napoleon destroyed the Arsenale in 1797, and although it was rebuilt by the Austrians, operations here ceased in 1917. The shipyard is now mainly used by the navy, although some of the buildings serve as exhibition space during La Biennale *(see box below)* and as a venue for the occasional theatre or concert. At the entrance visitors can only admire the impres-

La Biennale

Venice's Biennale (www.labiennale.org) is one of the oldest, most important exhibitions of contemporary art in the world. Established in 1895 to celebrate a royal silver wedding anniversary, it has been held regularly ever since.

Nowadays it takes place in odd years, (the architectural Biennale is held on even years) between June and November. It is held in two main locations in Castello district – the Arsenale, where the restored Corderie (rope factory) is the main venue, and the Giardini Pubblici, where there are around 40 pavilions including the sizeable Palazzo delle Esposizioni. Each pavilion is sponsored by a different country, offering a chance for avant-garde art, often with wry political comment, to be displayed. At the last Biennale, in 2009, 77 countries exhibited.

sive 15th-century gateway, guarded by a motley collection of white stone lions, all stolen from ancient Greek sites. The two on the river side are believed to date back to the 6th century BC.

Museo Storico Navale

The nearest you will get to the spirit of the age is in the **Museo Storico Navale** (Naval History Museum; Mon–Fri 8.45am–1.30pm, Sat morning only; charge). For many visitors the star attraction is the model of the last *Bucintoro*, the gilded barge that was used by the doge on state occasions, although entire sections of

Lion guarding the Arsenale

other state barges and warships are also on show. Don't miss the atmospheric annexe housed in the old **naval sheds** close to the Arsenale entrance, on the right-hand side of the river, where a range of ships is on display.

Unless you're heading for the Biennale exhibition *(see box opposite)* there's little of sightseeing interest further east along the waterfront. It's worth coming this far, however, simply for the splendid views back towards the Palazzo Ducale.

Scuola di San Giorgio degli Schiavoni

Returning to La Pietà *(see page 45)*, take the alley beside the church, turn right at Salizzada dei Greci and left after the canal for the **Scuola di San Giorgio degli Schiavoni** (Tue–Sat

9.15am–1pm, 2.45–6pm, Mon 2.45–6pm, Sun 9.15am–1pm; charge). The five Venetian *scuole* were craft guilds of laymen under the banner of a particular saint, and this one was founded in 1451 as the guildhall of the city's Dalmatian merchants. In the early 16th century these Slavs *(Schiavoni)*, prospering from trade with the East, commissioned Vittorio Carpaccio to decorate their hall. His nine pictures, completed between 1502 and 1508, decorate the lower floor and depict the lives of the three Dalmatian patron saints: Jerome, Tryphone and George. Note Carpaccio's gory *St George and the Dragon*.

Santa Maria Formosa

Return to Salizzada dei Greci and follow the flow west across the Rio dei Greci for the Fondamenta dell'Osmarin. A right turn at Calle Rota will take you up to the lively **Campo Santa Maria Formosa** and the 15th-century church of the

Market stall in Campo Santa Maria Formosa

same name (Mon–Sat 10am–5pm; charge), which is noted for its altarpiece by Palma il Vecchio.

Santi Giovanni e Paolo (San Zanipolo)

Commonly known as **San Zanipolo** (names are often slurred together in the Venetian dialect), this church (Mon–Sat 7.30am–6.30pm, Sun varies, depending on services; charge) is one of the largest in Venice after San Marco, disputing second place with its great Gothic sister, the Frari *(see page 65)*. The church is located on Campo Santi Giovanni e Paolo, north of Campo Santa Maria Formosa, reached via the narrow Calle Lunga Santa Maria Formosa and Calle Trevisana. The huge brick church was completed in 1430 for the Dominican Order and is known nowadays as Venice's Pantheon, as such a large number of doges (25 in all) and dignitaries of the Republic lie within. Like the Frari, the church is cavernous, with graphic sculptures adorning its tombs. The church's treasures include an early polyptych by Giovanni Bellini in the right-hand nave.

San Zanipolo shares the *campo* with the late 15th-century **Scuola Grande di San Marco** (now a civic hospital) and a magnificent 15th-century equestrian **statue of Bartolomeo Colleoni** by Andrea Verrochio and Alessandro Leopardi. The subject is the mercenary military leader who worked in the service of Venice for many years and left a large legacy to the city on condition that his statue would be raised 'at the Square of San Marco'. The leaders of the Republic, who had never erected statues to any of their leaders or permitted cults of personality, wanted the legacy but could not conceive of erecting a statue to a mercenary soldier in Piazza San Marco. As a compromise, Colleoni's statue was placed in the square of the Scuola Grande di San Marco – the rather tenuous San Marco association presumably salved the municipal conscience.

Santa Maria dei Miracoli

Santa Maria dei Miracoli

West of Santi Giovanni e Paolo, hidden amid a warren of canals and houses, lies the pretty little church of **Santa Maria dei Miracoli** (Mon–Sat 10am–5pm; charge) a popular choice for Venetian weddings. Built from 1481 to 1489 by the Lombardos, a family of inventive stonemasons who also created the *trompe-l'oeil* facade of the Scuola Grande di San Marco, the church has exquisite marble veneers on its inner and outer walls and an arched ceiling decorated with 50 portraits of prophets and saints.

DORSODURO

'Dorsoduro' is a name with which few first-time visitors to Venice will be familiar, yet most will visit this *sestiere* to see the city's main art gallery, the Accademia, or the iconic Santa Maria della Salute church. Dorsoduro encompasses the section of Venice that lies just across the Grand Canal from San Marco. Its eastern boundary is marked by the Punta della Dogana; its northern one by the Rio Nuovo–Rio Foscari.

Dorsoduro is perhaps the most picturesque part of Venice. Within this quiet residential area are three of the city's finest art collections and the city's university.

The Accademia

9 The **Gallerie dell'Accademia** (Mon 8.15am–2pm, Tue–Sun 8.15am–7.15pm; www.gallerieaccademia.org; charge) is home to the most pre-eminent collection of Venetian art in existence and is the most-visited spot in the city after Piazza San Marco and the Palazzo Ducale. A maximum of 180 visitors are allowed in at any one time, so arrive early to avoid the queues or make a reservation (tel: 041-520 0345, www.gallerieaccademia.org). Restoration of the galleries is ongoing so certain works of art may not be on view.

The collection spans paintings from the 14th to the 18th centuries, arranged roughly chronologically in 24 rooms. Visitors with only a limited amount of time to spare can hardly expect to absorb all the riches displayed here, and it's sensible to be selective rather than try and see everything and take in nothing. The following summary of the museum's highlights should help you make the most of your visit.

Room 2 contains Carpaccio's striking *Crucifixion of the Ten Thousand Martyrs*, while **Room 4** draws crowds of art lovers for its exquisite paintings, including Mantegna's *St*

Tintoretto's *Transport of St Mark*, Accademia collection

George and a fine series of works by Giovanni Bellini and Giorgione. **Room 5** holds the most famous work of art in the gallery, Giorgione's moody and enigmatic *Tempest*; it also houses *Portrait of an Old Woman*, by the same artist.

In **Room 10** look out for Veronese's *Feast at the House of Levi*, a painting of a raucous Renaissance banquet originally entitled (and meant to depict) *The Last Supper*. When church officials condemned the work as sacrilegious and ordered Ver-

Venetian Artists

• **Jacopo Bellini** (1400–70) and his sons **Giovanni** (1430–1516) and **Gentile** (1429–1507) inaugurated the *Serenissima's* glorious era of art in the 15th century.

• The Venetian High Renaissance began with **Giorgione** (c.1477–1510), whose great promise can be seen in *Tempest*, at the Accademia.

• **Vittore Carpaccio** (1445–1526) painted detailed scenes of city life as well as the splendid series on the life of St Ursula at the Accademia.

• **Titian** (1490–1576) was widely hailed as the finest painter of his era. Only a few of his works can be seen in Venice; these include the *Assumption of the Virgin*, above the altar of the Frari church.

• **Jacopo Tintoretto** (1518–94) was a quiet, religious man who left Venice only once. Most of his work remains in the city. See his genius in the Scuola di San Rocco and his parish church of Madonna dell'Orto.

• **Paolo Veronese** (1528–88) is inextricably linked with the church of San Sebastiano, which is resplendent with his paintings. Many of his works are in the Accademia.

• **Antonio Canaletto** (1697–1768) is famed for his detailed paintings of Venice but only three are on show in the city – most were sold abroad by his English patron, Josef Smith.

• Perhaps the greatest Venetian decorative painter was **Giovanni Battista Tiepolo** (1696–1770), who covered the ceiling of the upper hall in the Scuola Grande dei Carmini with nine masterly paintings.

onese to change it, he blithely did nothing but change its name. Jacopo Tintoretto's dazzling St Mark paintings, notably the haunting *Transport of the Body of St Mark*, are also here, as is Titian's dark *Pietà*, the artist's last work, intended for his tomb. **Room 11** contains masterpieces by Veronese and Tintoretto, as well as Tiepolo's *Rape of Europa*, a triumph of pulsating light and shade, while **Room 17** contains a real rarity – the Accademia's only painting by Canaletto.

Detail from Carpaccio's St Ursula cycle, Accademia

Out of sequence, **Room 23** is housed in the top of the church that constitutes part of the gallery structure. The airy, spacious loft is the perfect setting for some splendid altarpieces, notably the faded but powerful *Blessed Lorenzo Giustinian* by Gentile Bellini. **Room 20** is probably the most stunning in the Accademia, with four immense paintings occupying one wall apiece. Gentile Bellini's celebrated *Procession Around the Piazza Bearing the Cross* reveals how little San Marco has changed since 1496, except for its mosaics and the addition of the Campanile and Procuratie Nuove. Other illustrious paintings include Carpaccio's epic *Miracle of the Holy Cross at the Rialto Bridge*, showing the old bridge at the Rialto *(see page 62)* and gondolas on the Grand Canal.

In **Room 21** is Carpaccio's lyrical, poetically narrative *St Ursula* cycle, which depicts the tragic life of this Breton heroine. It spans her acceptance of the hand of the British prince, Hereus, on condition of his conversion to Christianity, to

Henry Moore sculpture at the Collezione Peggy Guggenheim

their subsequent pilgrimage to Rome and eventual martyrdom at the hands of Attila the Hun.

On the second floor, the **Quadreria** (booking required, tel: 041-520 0345) is packed with yet more Venetian masterpieces.

Collezione Peggy Guggenheim

Just to the east of the Accademia along the Grand Canal, in the Palazzo Venier dei Leoni (see also page 77), is another exceptional museum, the **Collezione Peggy Guggenheim** (Wed–Mon 10am–6pm; www.guggenheim-venice.it; charge), which is generally regarded as one of the best and most comprehensive collections of modern art in Europe. The bequest of American expatriate and heiress Peggy Guggenheim, who died in 1979, is displayed in the building she made her home: an eccentrically designed, one-storey 18th-century palace (still unfinished), with its gardens and terrace overlooking the Grand Canal. Guggenheim was renowned for her hospitality, and the administrators of the Collezione have tried to make the museum especially welcoming. The museum café, with a menu designed by the owner of Ai Gondolieri, is one of the better restaurants in Venice.

Among the outstanding exhibits are early Picassos and Chagalls and Brancusi's bronze sculpture *Bird in Space*. Other highlights include works by Max Ernst (whom Guggenheim married), Dalí, Miró, Piet Mondrian and Jackson Pollock, as well as a sculpture by Calder that Guggenheim used in lieu of a headboard for her bed. Sculptures by Giacometti dot the garden. Don't miss Marino Marini's *Angel of the Citadel*, a bold, joyfully erotic bronze equestrian statue in the garden facing the Grand Canal.

La Salute

Having presided over the entrance to the Grand Canal for over 300 years, the magnificent baroque church of **Santa Maria della Salute** (daily 9am–noon, 3–5pm) is almost as familiar a Venetian landmark as the Basilica di San Marco. The church, popularly known among the Venetians as 'La Salute', was built as an offering of thanks to the Virgin Mary for the end of a catastrophic plague in 1630 – the plague wiped out over a third of the lagoon's inhabitants. Under the direction of the young architect, Baldassare Longhena, construction began in 1631 and more than one million oak pil-

La Salute bathed in evening light

ings were sunk into the swampy earth to support the massive structure. Longhena lived to see the church, his life's work, completed in 1682. Each year, on 21 November, the church's feast day (Festa della Salute), engineers build a great pontoon of boats over the Grand Canal, and most of the city's population, resident and visiting, join a procession across the water and into the church. This is the only day that the church's main doors are opened.

Inside, in the sacristy (charge) to the left of the high altar, is Tintoretto's magnificent painting of the *Marriage at Cana*. Three Titians (*Cain and Abel*, *Abraham Sacrificing Isaac* and *David and Goliath*) are also on view.

Dogana

Continue east from the Salute towards the tip of Dorsoduro. At this point you'll find the 17th-century **Dogana di Mare** (Customs House), where the cargos from all incoming ships were inspected in former days. The long-abandoned building has been converted by Japanese architect, Tadao Ando, into the **Punta della Dogana Contemporary Art Centre** (Wed–Mon 10am–7pm; charge) which has rotating displays of artworks from the world-class collection of François Pinault, owner of the Palazzo Grassi (*see page* 76; combined ticket available). Atop the tower of the Dogana is the curious balletic wind-vane showing the figure of Fortune (also possibly representing justice), holding a ship's rudder and set on a large gilded globe supported by two Atlas-like figures.

The views from here, looking straight into the Bacino di San Marco (St Mark's Basin) in one direction and across the **Canale della Giudecca** (Giudecca Canal) in the other, are among the most breathtaking in the whole city. From the Punta della Dogana look out across the Canale della Giudecca to the islands of Giudecca and San Giorgio Maggiore; this vista takes in three churches designed by Andrea Palladio:

Looking towards the Punta della Dogana

the imposing church of **San Giorgio Maggiore** *(see page 78)*, **Le Zitelle** (the Church of the Spinsters) and the grand church of the **Redentore** (Redeemer). The last was built, like the Salute after it, as an act of thanksgiving at the end of the devastating plague of 1575–6. As at the Salute, there is an annual celebration at the Redentore each third Sunday of July; the festivities culminate in a flotilla of small boats and a spectacular display of fireworks over the water.

Zattere

The **Fondamente delle Zattere** (Quay of the Rafts), runs all the way along the southern waterfront from the Dogana to the Rio di San Sebastiano. The floating rafts that gave the Zattere its name were once major unloading points for cargoes of salt and other such valuable commodities. The huge salt warehouse, once capable of storing over 40,000 tons of the mineral, is now partly used as a boathouse for a local rowing club.

Continue along the Zattere past the churches of Spirito Santo and the Gesuati (Santa Maria del Rosario). Turn right on to the Fondamenta Nani and a few yards further along on the opposite side you will see the rustic **Squero di San Trovaso** (*squero* means boatyard). In the 16th century, when thousands of gondolas plied the waters, there were many *squeri*; nowadays, just four remain in operation, and San Trovaso is the only one where you can see gondolas and other craft waiting to be repaired. The church of **San Trovaso** (Mon–Sat 3–5pm) is worth investigating for two of Tintoretto's last works, both completed by his son.

Head back to the Zattere, which, with its cafés and restaurants, is a good place to take a break. The huge red-

Gondolas and Gondoliers

Nothing is more quintessentially Venetian than the gondola, although nowadays they are more a tourist attraction than a means of transportation. Gondolas have existed since the 11th century, and in the 18th century around 14,000 plied Venice's canals; today, the number has fallen to 400.

All gondolas are made to the same specifications, built by hand from around 280 separate pieces of wood. Curiously, they are asymmetrical (the left side is wider than the right) in order to accommodate the gondolier as he rows and steers. Gondolas are painted black in deference to the sumptuary laws of 1562 that attempted to curb the extravagances of Venetian society. They also retain a rather curious metallic pronged prow (or *ferro*). Several explanations have been offered for the symbolism and shape of the *ferro*: some think that the blades represent the six districts of Venice; others maintain that the shape suggests the Grand Canal or even the doge's cap.

Many gondoliers still wear the traditional outfit of straw boater, striped T-shirt and white sailor's top, although these days, if you want to be serenaded, that will cost extra.

brick landmark that you can see across the water right at the western end of Giudecca is the **Molino Stucky** (Stucky's Mill), a flour mill that was part of an attempt to bring modern industry to Venice in the 1890s. It closed in 1954 and was abandoned for 50 years. After major renovations the building opened in 2007 as the five-star Hilton Molino

Classic gondolier garb

Stucky, with 380 rooms, Venice's largest congress centre and a rooftop swimming pool with sublime views.

Turn right along the waterfront and, at the San Basilio landing stage, head inland, following the canal north. Cross the tiny bridge for the splendid 16th-century church of **San Sebastiano** (Mon–Sat 10am–5pm, Sun 1–5pm; charge). It is a glittering tribute to Veronese, who painted most of the opulent works decorating the walls, altar and ceiling from 1555 to 1565. The artist is also buried here.

The next square west is Campo Angelo Raffaele, named after its 17th century church. The adjoining canal leads to the humble parish church of **San Nicolò dei Mendicoli** (daily 10am–noon, 4–6pm) – often overlooked, but its relatively modest exterior belies its lavishly decorated interior. The church was founded in the 7th century, making it one of the oldest in the city, and remodelled between the 12th and 14th centuries; it was sensitively restored in 1977 by the Venice in Peril Fund. The church's single nave is graced by Romanesque columns, Gothic capitals and beamed ceilings, while decoration includes Renaissance panelling, gilded statues and paintings from the School of Veronese.

Campo Santa Margherita is lively at night

The University Quarter

The attractive area between the Accademia and Campo Santa Margherita is pervaded (but not dominated) by the city's University. In term time **Campo Santa Margherita**, home to numerous inexpensive restaurants, bohemian shops and colourful market stalls, is the liveliest square in Venice outside Piazza San Marco. At one end of the square is the restored church of **Santa Margherita**, while at the other end is the spacious and ornately decorated **Chiesa dei Carmini** (Church of the Carmelites). For even more religious art, call in next door at **I Carmini** (Mar–Oct daily 10am–5pm, Nov–Feb Thur–Tue 11am–4pm; charge), the headquarters of the Scuola Grande dei Carmini and a showcase for the work of Tiepolo, who covered the ceiling of the Upper Hall with nine paintings, the last one completed in 1744.

From Campo Santa Margherita the Rio Terrà street leads southeast towards **Campo San Barnaba** which sits on the other side of San Barnaba canal. Here you'll see an attractive fruit-and-vegetable barge moored along the quay, and the solemn, Neo-Classical church of **San Barnaba**, which film buffs may recognise as the setting for major scenes in *Summertime* (with Katharine Hepburn) and *Indiana Jones and the Last Crusade*.

Ca' Rezzonico

On the other side of the San Barnaba canal where it meets the Grand Canal is the glorious 17th-century **Ca' Rezzonico** (Wed–Mon 10am–6pm, 5pm in winter; charge), home to the **Museo del Settecento Veneziano** (Museum of 18th-Century Venice), another of Dorsoduro's major art collections. Here, however, the 17th-century palatial setting is just as important as the 18th-century exhibits it houses.

Stepping into the Ca' Rezzonico is a feast for the eyes. At the top of the vast entrance staircase is a stunning ballroom, featuring two immense Murano-glass chandeliers as well as vibrantly decorated ceilings and walls. In the adjacent room are intricately carved figures of chained slaves.

Ceilings by Tiepolo (father and son) are the main artistic interest until you reach the gallery on the second floor. Most visitors are immediately drawn to the two Canaletto paintings of the Grand Canal – there are only three paintings by him in the whole of Venice. You'll also find works by Pietro Longhi, who recorded the final, decadent century of the Venetian Republic. On the third and fourth floors of the museum, the Gallery Egidio Martini showcases an impressive collection of around 300 works, mainly by Venetian painters.

The views from the windows overlooking the Grand Canal are also to be savoured. Pen Browning, the son of poet Robert Browning owned this palace in the late 19th century, and his father died here in 1889. The American-born artist James Whistler also lived here from 1879 to 1880.

SAN POLO AND SANTA CROCE

The two adjoining *sestieri* of San Polo and Santa Croce are curved into the left bank of the Grand Canal. Together they are home to many important sights, including the artistic treasure houses of the church of the Frari and the Scuola Grande di San Rocco, as well as one of the city's most vibrant attractions: the Rialto markets.

The Rialto

Not only Venice's oldest district, the **Rialto** is also the area of the city with the greatest concentration of Veneto-Byzantine palaces. From its earliest foundation, this was the powerhouse of the Republic, and a crossroads between the East and the West. On a practical level, it also acted as a busy commercial exchange and meeting place for merchants. As such, it is often described as 'Venice's kitchen, office and back parlour'. During the peak of the Republic's influence it was one of the most important financial centres in Europe (reflected in Shakespeare's *Merchant of Venice*, when Shylock asks of Bassanio, 'What news on the Rialto?').

Ponte di Rialto

14 ▶ The **Ponte di Rialto** (Rialto Bridge) traditionally divides the city into two, with the right bank, on the San Marco side, known as the *Rialto di quà* (this side), and the left bank known as the *Rialto di là* (that side). The bridge spans the Grand Canal with a strong, elegantly curved arch of marble, and is lined with shops selling silk ties, scarves, leather and jewellery. Henry James appreciated the 'small shops and booths that abound in Venetian character' but also felt 'the communication of insect life'.

The current bridge is merely the last in a line that began with simple pontoons and then progressed to a wooden struc-

Ponte di Rialto

ture, with a drawbridge section to allow the passage of tall ships. A new bridge was created in 1588–91 by Antonio da Ponte following the collapse of the previous one. Tradition has it that the greatest architects of the day, including Michelangelo and Palladio, competed for the commission, but da Ponte's design was chosen. The result is a light, floating structure with shops nestling in its solid, closed arches. From the bridge one can admire the majestic sweep of palaces and warehouses swinging away to La Volta del Canal, the great elbow-like bend in the Grand Canal.

The Rialto Markets

The other highlight of the Rialto is its **markets**, which make ◀ **15** a refreshing change from the monumental Venice of San Marco. Ignore the tourist tat in favour of foodstuffs galore – as well as the markets the area is home to some excellent food shops and *bacari* (traditional Venetian wine bars).

Brightly painted boats supply
produce to the Pescheria

The **Erberia** is a fruit-and-vegetable market over-looking the Grand Canal. Casanova spoke of it as a place for 'innocent pleasure', but latter-day foodies might find sensuous pleasure in the profusion of medicinal herbs, flowers, fruit and local vegetables – from asparagus and radicchio to baby artichokes – on offer here.

The markets extend along the bank to the **Pescheria**, the fish market, set in an arcaded neo-Gothic hall by the quayside, a design inspired by Carpaccio's realistic paintings. Under the porticos, fishermen set their catch on mountains of ice. The adjoining **Campo delle Beccarie**, once a public abattoir, now contains market overspill and a lively bar and restaurant.

Campo San Polo

The biggest square in the city outside Piazza San Marco, **Campo San Polo** is notable for its church and for the mid-14th-century rose-coloured **Palazzo Soranzo**, situated just opposite. Casanova came to this palace in the 18th century as a young, hired violinist, living as the adopted son and heir to the family fortune with access to the very best of Venetian society. From here, he went on to seduce and outrage the world of Europe's 18th-century aristocracy.

16▶ Note the fine portal of the church of **San Polo** (Mon–Sat 10am–5pm; charge), one of the few features that survives from the original 15th-century building. The interior, reached through a side door, features a brooding *Last Supper* by Tintoretto and Giandomenico Tiepolo's *Via Crucis (Stations of the Cross)* painted when he was only 20 years old. A campanile, dating from 1362, stands a short way from the church and is adorned with two of the Republic's less-appealing lions, one playing with a human head, the other with a serpent.

The Frari

Santa Maria Gloriosa dei Frari (known simply as the Frari, a deformation of *frati*, meaning 'brothers'; Mon–Sat 9am–6pm, Sun 1–6pm; charge) is Venice's second church after San Marco and the resting place of the painter Titian. The brothers in question – members of the Franciscan order – were granted a piece of land in 1236, and the church, a huge lofty structure, was rebuilt between 1340 and 1469.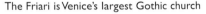

The church's greatest treasure is the soaring, mysterious *Assumption* (1518) hanging in the Gothic apse above the high

The Friari is Venice's largest Gothic church

> **Titian's wife**
>
> Before you leave the Frari church, be sure to note the splendid *Madonna di Ca' Pesaro* by Titian, which is thought to represent the artist's wife.

altar. One of Titian's early masterpieces, this painting helped to establish his reputation. To the right is Donatello's much-admired wooden statue of *St John the Baptist*. Restored during the 19th century, it is the Florentine artist's sole remaining work in Venice. Tucked away in the sacristy on the right is the *Madonna and Saints* (1488), a triptych by Giovanni Bellini. Don't miss the beautiful marquetry and intricate carving on the choir stalls – this choir is one of the few in Venetian churches to stand in its original location.

The Frari is also notable for its huge monuments to Titian and to the 19th-century sculptor, Canova, on opposite sides of the great nave. Although Titian was buried here in 1576, the monument to him was not built until the mid-19th century. Canova's mausoleum was erected in 1827, five years after his death; however, only his heart is interred here.

Several doges are entombed in the Frari, including two in the high altar. The church is also home to one of the city's most bombastic monuments, which is dedicated to Doge Giovanni Pesaro and situated next to Canova's mausoleum.

Scuola Grande di San Rocco

18 The nearby **Scuola Grande di San Rocco** (daily 9am–5.30pm, 5pm off season; charge) stirs the emotions. John Ruskin, the foremost Venetian art historian of the 19th century and one of the city's most scrupulous observers, described San Rocco as having one of the three most precious picture collections in all Italy (ranking it above the Accademia). The novelist Henry James was also a devotee, although he found the Scuola Grande a little too breathtaking, proclaiming it to be 'suffocating'.

In 1564 Tintoretto won a competition to decorate the interior, and for the next 23 years much of his time was spent painting the 65 pictures here. The artist began upstairs in the sumptuous **Sala dell' Albergo**, just off the main hall, so make your way straight there before coming back down to the lower hall. On the ceiling is Tintoretto's *The Glory of St Roch*, which was the work that won him the commission. His monumental *Crucifixion* in the same room (described by Ruskin as 'beyond all analysis and above all praise') is said to have been considered by the artist to be his greatest painting.

In the dimly lit main hall, the gilded **ceiling** is covered with 21 immense pictures, and there are another 13 on the walls (all of which are captioned on the helpful plan provided free at the entrance). The best way of studying the ceiling works is to focus on the detail, rather than attempting to take in broad sweeps at once. Hidden in the gloom below the murals are some wonderful, if slightly odd, wooden figures by Venice's off-beat 17th-century sculptor Francesco Pianto.

In contrast to the pictures in the main hall, those on the ground floor (representing scenes from the life of the Virgin) seem almost playful. Look out for *The Flight into Egypt*, widely acknowledged

Tintoretto's *The Glory of St Roch*, Scuola Grande di San Rocco

Fondaco dei Turchi illuminated at night

as another of Tintoretto's great paintings. More Tintorettos are on display in the church of San Rocco next door.

Casa di Carlo Goldoni

Close to Campo San Polo and the Frari is the **Casa di Carlo Goldoni** (daily, Apr–Oct 10am–5pm, Nov–Mar 10am–4pm; charge), the house in which the playwright Carlo Goldoni was born in 1707. In 1952 the house was turned into a small museum dedicated to the writer and his works, and although the contents are quite specialist, the house is worth a visit for its well-preserved Gothic architecture, especially its handsome courtyard.

Fondaco dei Turchi

The main route north from Campo di San Polo brings you into the large, rambling Campo San Giacomo dell'Orio. From here follow the Calle Larga and Fondamenta del Megio for the **Fondaco dei Turchi**, built in 1227 but now home to the  **Museo di Storia Naturale** (Natural History Museum; currently being restored and only partially open, Tue–Fri 9am–1pm, Sat–Sun 10am–4pm; tel: 041-520 9070), which is a rather old-fashioned collection but still popular with children.

Among the more terrifying exhibits are a monster crab with legs 2m (6½ft) long and a scorpion over 30cm (1ft) long. The most impressive exhibits, however, are in the dinosaur room, notably the bones of possibly the largest extinct crocodilian creatures ever found (11m/37ft in length) and the complete skeleton of a massive biped reptile known as an *ouranosaurus* (almost 3.5m/12ft high and some 7m/23ft long).

Ca' Pesaro

Zigzag your way east for the next museum on the Grand Canal, the **Galleria Internazionale d'Arte Moderna**, beyond the San Stae landing stage (Tue–Sun, Apr–Oct 10am–6pm, Nov–Mar 10am–5pm; charge), housed in the baroque **Ca' Pesaro**. The gallery was founded with the best of the Biennale exhibition pieces and features mainly Italian artists, with a few important international contemporary works.

Upstairs in the same building is the **Museo d'Arte Orientale** (same opening times as above), a rather confusing jumble of lacquered pieces, Samurai arms and armour and other artefacts given to Venice by Austria after World War I as reparation for bombing attacks on the city.

Rodin statue in the Galleria Internazionale d'Arte Moderna

Star of David in the Ghetto

CANNAREGIO

This district, close to the railway station, is the most northerly one in Venice. Its name comes from *canne*, meaning reeds, indicating its marshy origins. This is an ancient quarter, often scorned by the snobbish in favour of the more stylish Dorsoduro – ironically, this was once one of the city's most fashionable spots, dotted with foreign embassies and palatial gardens. The palaces may be faded, but Cannaregio remains both a retreat for cognoscenti and the last bastion for working-class Venetians who have not moved to the Mestre mainland. It is also the site of the world's first Jewish ghetto.

The Ghetto

For almost 300 years, until Napoleon ended the practice in 1797, the Jews of Venice were permitted to live only in this tiny section of Cannaregio, surrounded on all sides by canals. The area had previously been a foundry or *ghetto* in Venetian; the word 'ghetto' subsequently came to denote Jewish and other segregated quarters all over the world.

Jewish refugees fleeing the War of Cambrai in 1508 came in their thousands to settle here. At the Ghetto's peak in the 17th century, its inhabitants numbered some 5,000, and the limited space led to the building of tenements six storeys high (still tall for Venice). Venetian Jews were severely taxed, forced to wear distinctive clothing, barred from many professions and made to observe a curfew, which was strictly enforced by watchmen.

However, by the 16th century, the Ghetto was flourishing, with choirs, theatrical groups and literary salons that were visited by non-Jewish Venetians. The market at the Campo del Ghetto was the lively 'pawnshop of Venice' – an international attraction where treasures from the great houses of Venice's recently bankrupt or dead were bought and sold.

Today, the Ghetto is a quiet residential corner of Venice, with only a small Jewish population, though the area is rich in Jewish culture with restaurants, bakeries and shops selling Jewish handicrafts. The **Museo Ebraico** (Jewish Museum; June–Sept Sun–Fri 10am–7pm, Oct–May until 5.30pm; charge) o Campo del Ghetto Nuovo contains a remarkable collection of Italian Judaica and runs tours of synagogues in the area every hour from 10.30am–4.30pm. On the opposite side of the square, a series of reliefs commemorates the 202 Venetian Jews who died in World War II.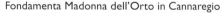

Fondamenta Madonna dell'Orto in Cannaregio

Madonna dell'Orto

22 The 15th-century church of the **Madonna dell'Orto** (Our Lady of the Garden; Mon–Sat 10am–5pm; charge) occupies a quiet spot northeast of the Ghetto. After crossing the canal north of the Campo di Ghetto Nuovo, follow the bank east before turning left onto Calle Larga and continuing north through the Campo dei Mori.

The church, which has a delicate Gothic facade and lovely cloister, was built to house a miraculous statue of the Virgin and Child, found in a nearby garden *(orto)*. However, it is best known nowadays for its connections with the Renaissance painter Tintoretto – this was his parish church, and he is buried with his family to the right of the choir, near the high altar. The church is filled with Tintoretto's paintings, including his *Last Judgement*, *The Worship of the Golden Calf* and the *Presentation of the Virgin* (over the sacristy door), which demonstrates the artist's typical theatricality and grandiosity. Also of interest is Cima da Conegliano's remarkable painting of *St John the Baptist*, to the right of the entrance.

Ca' d'Oro

Head south from the Madonna dell'Orto towards the Strada
23 Nova, which leads east to the **Ca' d'Oro**, the finest Venetian Gothic palace in the city, which is best viewed from the Grand Canal *(see page 75)*. Inside is the **Galleria Franchetti** (Mon 8.15am–2pm, Tue–Sun 8.15am–7.15pm; charge), home to Mantegna's gruesome *St Sebastian*, depicting the saint riddled with arrows, some notable Renaissance sculpture, minor paintings by Tintoretto and Titian, and remnants of frescos recovered from other buildings, including some by Giorgione.

> ### The 'little dyer'
>
> Tintoretto (1518–94), who spent his whole life in Venice, was nicknamed after his father's trade as a dyer.

A gilded gondola

BOAT TRIP ALONG THE GRAND CANAL

The extraordinary main artery through Venice, the **Grand Canal** (Canal Grande) – or *Canalazzo*, as it is known to the locals – stretches over 4km (2 miles), from inauspicious beginnings near the Stazione Ferrovia (railway station) to a glorious final outpouring into the Basino di San Marco (St Mark's Basin). The views along the canal are so wonderful that many visitors ride the *vaporetti* back and forth for hours, soaking up the atmosphere; a good waterbus to take is the inappropriately named *accelerato* (No. 1), which stops at every landing stage.

The banks of the canal are lined with more than 200 ornate palaces and grand houses, most built between the 14th and 18th centuries. While some have been superbly restored, others have a neglected air, awaiting their turn for renovation. Very few of these homes are still inhabited by

Ponte di Calatrava

After four years of delay and controversy the new Calatrava Bridge was installed over the Grand Canal in September 2008. The fourth bridge over the famous canal links Piazzale Roma with the railway station, and is named after its Spanish architect, Santiago Calatrava. Most Venetians see the glass and steel structure as incongruous and superfluous to needs. The issue of access for the disabled has also given rise to major controversy.

the aristocratic families for whom they were built; the majority have been turned into offices, hotels, apartments or gallery spaces.

The following section details some of the most outstanding palaces to look for while travelling along the canal from the railway station (Stazione Ferrovia) towards Piazza San Marco.

Fondaco dei Turchi to the Ca' d'Oro

The first building of note on the right bank is the **Fondaco dei Turchi**, which is home to the Natural History Museum *(see page 69)*. Built in Veneto-Byzantine style in 1227 (though brutally restored in the 19th century), it is one of the Grand Canal's oldest survivors, once a trading base and living quarters for Turkish merchants.

Just beyond the San Marcuola landing stage on the left bank is the **Palazzo Vendramin-Calergi**, designed by Mauro Coducci (1440–1504). The German composer Richard Wagner died here in 1883 and his apartments are open to visitors (Tue and Sat 10.30am, Thur 2.30pm, booking required, tel: 338-416 4174); the building also provides an opulent setting for Venice's Casino *(see pages 91–2)*.

Beyond the San Stae stop on the right bank is the vast baroque **Ca' Pesaro**, designed by Baldassare Longhena (the architect of the Salute). Decorated with grotesque masks, the Ca' (short for 'Casa', or house) was completed in 1682 and is now home to two art museums *(see page 69)*.

By the next landing stage is the **Ca' d'Oro** (home to the Galleria Franchetti, *see page 72*), built in the first quarter of the 15th century for the wealthy patrician Marino Contarini. The Ca' was originally covered in gold leaf, hence its name, which means 'House of Gold'. It is one of the most famous frontages on the Grand Canal, renowned for its elaborate Gothic facade decorated with magnificent tracery.

Past the Rialto

Just north of the Rialto, on the left bank, stands the 13th-century Veneto-Byzantine-style **Ca' da Mosto**, one of the oldest houses on the canal. Nearby is the landmark **Ponte di Rialto** (Rialto Bridge, *see page 62*). Also on the left bank, to the south, are the handsome twin 13th-century *palazzi* **Loredan** and **Farsetti**, which now function as the town hall. After the San Silvestro stop, on the right bank is the

The magnificent facade of the Ca' d'Oro

View along the Grand Canal

splendid mid-13th century **Palazzo Bernardo**, which may look familiar, since its tracery mirrors that of the Palazzo Ducale.

Around the Bend

Opposite the San Tomà stop is the **Palazzo Mocenigo** complex, marked by blue-and-white mooring posts *(pali)*. The poet Lord Byron lived here from 1819 to 1824, while balancing the needs of a number of fiery local mistresses and working on his mock-heroic narrative poem *Don Juan*. Byron's most daring Venetian venture was to swim in a race against two other men from the Lido *(see page 86)* all the way to the Rialto – an excellent swimmer, the poet was the only one to finish. Today, the Grand Canal is no longer clean enough for such aquatic feats.

On the bend of the canal, on the opposite side, look out for three attractive palaces: the **Balbi** (1590), then the **Ca' Foscari** (1437), currently home to the university, and finally the **Giustinian** (*c*.1452), where Wagner composed part of his opera *Tristan and Isolde*.

Located a few blocks on is the glorious 17th-century **Ca' Rezzonico**, home to the Museo del Settecento Veneziano *(see page 61)*. Opposite is the 18th-century **Palazzo Grassi** (Wed–Mon 10am–7pm; charge) which in 2005 was bought by the French magnate, François Pinault, to house his magnificent collection of contemporary art. The palace can only accommodate a fraction of the vast collection; it is also used as a centre for major international art exhibitions.

Ponte dell'Accademia to La Salute

A little further on, the **Ponte dell'Accademia** (Accademia Bridge) was built as a temporary wooden arch in 1932, replacing an iron structure erected by the Austrians that had become an obstruction to larger *vaporetti*. The bridge has fine views towards the Salute church.

The splendid building to the left, with the classic red-and-white *pali*, is the 15th-century **Palazzo Cavalli Franchetti**, while the neighbouring **Palazzo Barbaro**, built from the 15th to the 17th centuries, was much favoured by the artistic and literary set – writers Robert Browning and Henry James, and artists John Singer Sargent, Claude Monet and James Whistler all spent time here.

Next en route is the right bank's **Palazzo Barbarigo**, decorated with strikingly gaudy, late-19th-century mosaics. Close by, the one-storey **Palazzo Venier dei Leoni** is home to the Collezione Peggy Guggenheim *(see page 54)*. The final building to note as you head along the canal towards its mouth is the gently listing 15th-century **Ca' Dario** (or Palazzo Dario), the former home of the Venetian chancery secretary, Giovanni Dario. Five centuries of scandal, from suicides to bankruptcy to suspicious deaths, have plagued the house. Note its funnel-shaped chimney pots, designed to reduce the risk of fire.

Life on the canal

'A man's life often resembles these palaces on the Grand Canal, which begin at the base with an array of stones proudly sculpted in diamond points, and end with the upper floors hastily cobbled together from dry mud.'

Paul Morand

San Giorgio Maggiore

THE ISLANDS

A highlight of any visit to Venice is a *vaporetto* trip through the inviting lagoon. Although many of its small islands are un-inhabited wildernesses, inaccessible by public transport, there is a range of others to visit, from glass-making Murano to colourful Burano and serene Torcello. Here are some suggestions for leisurely half-day or one-day island excursions.

San Giorgio Maggiore

24 ▶ **San Giorgio Maggiore** is the closest island to the city, located almost within swimming distance of the Palazzo Ducale. The only major island of the lagoon that is untouched by commerce, it is home to a magnificent Palladian church/monastery and celebrated for the glorious views it affords back over the lagoon towards Venice. To reach the island, take the No 82 *vaporetto*; the journey lasts little more than 5 minutes.

Palladio's church (daily 9.30am–12.30pm, 2.30–6.30pm, until 4.30pm in winter) was completed in 1610, and the result is a masterpiece of proportion and harmonious space. Tintoretto's *Last Supper* and *The Gathering of Manna* (both 1592–4) grace either side of the chancel. The high altar is dominated by a large bronze group by Girolamo Campagna and represents the evangelists sustaining the world. Behind are the church's splendidly carved 16th-century choir stalls.

For most visitors, however, the church takes second place to the view from its 200-year-old campanile (charge). Take the lift to the top for one of the great panoramas of Venice, then look down into the cloister of the **monastery** below to see a rare grassy space. The Fondazione Cini occupies much of the monastic complex. Guided tours take place hourly at weekends (10am–4.30pm; charge), covering the library, refectory, cloisters and Teatro Verde, the open-air theatre.

San Michele

The island of **San Michele** is the site of the city's cemetery, hence its sombre nickname, the 'island of the dead'. It lies 400m/yds from Fondamente Nuove and is accessed by *vaporetti* Nos 41 and 42, which stop right outside **San**

Rest in Peace?

Nowhere is Venice's chronic lack of available land brought home so vividly as on the cemetery island of San Michele. In the early 1800s Napoleon decreed that burials should no longer take place in the city, and on San Michele they are not so much welcomed as tolerated. Burial lasts for ten years only, however, and unless the deceased has made provision for an extension on his or her lease – something that few Venetians can afford – then at the end of that time the remains are exhumed and sent to an ossuary to make way for the next occupant.

Michele in Isola, an elegant Renaissance church clad in glistening white Istrian stone.

Go through the cloister to reach the **cemetery** (daily, Apr–Sept 7.30am–6pm, Oct–Mar 7.30am–4pm). Among the cypress trees, you can visit the graves of American poet Ezra Pound (1885–1972), in section XV, and composer Igor Stravinsky (1882–1971) and impresario Serge Diaghilev (1872–1929), in section XIV.

Murano

After San Michele, the *vaporetti* stop at **Murano**, an island long famed for its glass-blowing tradition. Free water-taxi excursions are offered by glass factories or hotels, but if you want to avoid high-pressure sales tactics once you're on the island, take the *vaporetto* and make your own way around the factories instead. Orientation in Murano is a simple matter. From the main quay, where you disembark at the Colonna *vaporetto* stop, stroll along the picturesque Fondamenta dei Vetrai, which leads to Murano's very own Grand Canal.

Although glass was manufactured in Venice as far back as the 10th century, the open furnaces presented such a fire hazard that c.1292 the Republic ordered the factories to be transferred to Murano. Grouped here, the glass blowers kept the secrets of their trade for centuries; the manufacture of mirrors, for instance, was for a long time exclusive to Venice.

The island prospered, and by the early 16th century its population reached some 30,000. Glass artisans were considered honoured citizens. Murano's crystalware decorated royal palaces abroad,

Clear vision

It is thought that the Muranesi were the first to invent spectacles, in the early 14th century. By that time they were renowned for their window panes, which were the largest and clearest in Europe.

Contemporary Murano glass

and its sumptuous villas housed the leading nobles and diplomats of the city. In time, as other countries learned and applied the secrets of Murano's glass-making, the island's importance declined, and by the 19th century most of its grand summer residences were no more. However, the glass industry was revived later that century and continues today, though not always up to the old standards and often at over-inflated prices. However, a number of contemporary glass workshops still create outstanding designs.

For an interesting review of the history of Venetian glass, visit the **Museo del Vetro** (Glass Museum; Thur–Tue, Apr–Oct 10am–5pm, Nov–Mar 10am–4pm; charge), housed in a 17th-century bishop's palace on Fondamente Giustinian.

Nearby, on Campo San Donato, is the church of **Santi Maria e Donato** (Mon–Sat 9am–noon, 3.30–7pm), which is possibly the oldest church in Venice – its 7th-century foundations may predate the Basilica di San Marco. The church is

Symbol of the island

splendidly atmospheric, and both the brightly coloured 12th-century mosaic floor and a golden mosaic of the Madonna over the high altar have been restored with great care and sympathy. While you're in the church, note the giant bones behind the altar; these are said to be those of a dragon slain by St Donato. Unlike St George, Donato eschewed the conventional lance and sword, slewing the beast simply by spitting at it.

Burano

The LN (Laguna Nord) ferry service to **Burano** leaves roughly every half hour from Venice's Fondamente Nuove; those visiting from Murano can pick the ferry up at the Faro (lighthouse) stop. The journey to Burano and the neighbouring island of Torcello takes around 45 minutes.

Burano is a friendly, colourful island which feels like an authentic old fishing village. Its buildings are painted in a rainbow of blue, red, peppermint, russet and yellow, and these colours all reflect in the waters of the canals. You won't need a map here – it's such a small place that you're unlikely to get lost if you use the campanile of San Martino as your reference point.

The island once produced the world's finest lace, and its exquisitely light *punto in aria* pattern was the most sought after in Europe. Nowadays, the lace you see in local shops is largely imported from Asia, and real Burano lace is created by only a handful of women trained at the island's lacemaking school, now the **Museo del Merletto** (Museum of Lacemaking; Wed–Mon 10am–5pm, until 4pm in winter; charge), on Piazza Galuppi. The school was opened in 1872 to re-train the island's women at a time when the numbers of skilled lacemakers had dwindled to just one.

Before leaving the square, visit the 16th-century church of **San Martino** (daily 8am–noon, 3–6pm), famous for its 18th-century leaning campanile. San Martino is also home to the island's only major art treasure: Tiepolo's *Crucifixion*.

San Francesco del Deserto

From Burano, the peaceful island of **San Francesco del Deserto** makes a lovely detour. The trip takes about 20 minutes and can normally be arranged with a boatman on Burano's main square. St Francis is said to have landed on the island in 1220, on his return from the Holy Land, and Franciscan

Burano waterfront

friars have been here almost ever since. A handful of the brethren choose to make this a permanent home, while young novices spend a year here as part of their training. The monastery (Tue–Sun 9–11am, 3–5pm; www.isola-sanfrancescodel deserto.it) has a beautiful 14th-century cloister and gardens.

Torcello

From Burano it's a mere 5-minute hop on the T ferry to the remote and evocative island of **Torcello**. Amazing as it seems now, in early medieval times this overgrown, almost deserted island was the lagoon's principal city, with an estimated population of 20,000. However, with the silting up of its canals into marshes, a consequent outbreak of malaria and then the ascendancy of Venice, there was a mass exodus from the island. Today, there are only about 50 inhabitants on Torcello.

Mosaic, Santa Maria dell'Assunta

As you walk from the *vaporetto* stage to the cathedral, the canal is the only familiarly Venetian feature. On Torcello, buildings have given way to trees, fields and thick undergrowth. The novelist George Sand captured the pastoral mood of her visit in the 1830s, 'Torcello is a reclaimed wilderness. Through copses of water willow and hibiscus bushes run saltwater streams where petrel and teal delight to stalk.'

The solitary path leads past the ancient **Ponte del Diavolo** to a small square where Torcello's cathedral, the adjacent church of Santa Fosca and the Museo di Torcello (Torcello Museum) all stand. The Italian-Byzantine cathedral **Santa Maria dell'Assunta** (daily 10.30am–6pm, 5pm in winter and on Sun; charge, collective ticket available) was founded in AD639, but dates mostly from 1008, and is therefore the oldest monument in the lagoon. Among the cathedral's treasures is its original 7th-century altar and a Roman sarcophagus containing the relics of St Heliodorus, first Bishop of Altinum (where the island's first settlers were originally from).

Also among the cathedral's highlights are its rich **mosaics**, judged by many to be the finest in Italy outside those at Ravenna. A masterpiece of Byzantine design adorns the central apse: a slender, mysterious *Madonna*, bathed in a cloth of gold. At the opposite end of the building, an entire wall is covered by a complex, heavily restored *Last Judgement*, probably begun early in the 12th century. The steep climb up the campanile will reward you with a panoramic view of the lagoon.

Santa Fosca (Mon–Sat 10am–4.30pm), built in the 11th and 12th centuries and harmoniously combining Romanesque and Byzantine elements, has a bare simplicity rarely found in Venetian churches, while the **Museo della Provincia** (Tue–Sun 10am–5pm, until 4.30 in winter) houses a collection of architectural details from long-disappeared local churches and other buildings. Outside the museum is a primitive stone chair, known as 'Attila's Throne'; it is possibly an early judge's seat.

The Lido

The long strip of land, sandwiched between the city of Venice and the waters of the Adriatic, belongs neither to Venice nor the mainland. This reflects the prime function of the **Lido**: to protect Venice from the engulfing tides. In spirit, it is a place apart, not quite a traditional summer resort nor a residential suburb. After the time warp of historic Venice, the sight of cars, villas and department stores can be disconcerting. Yet there is a touch of unreality about the Lido, hence its frequent role as a film set. In this faded fantasy, neo-Gothic piles vie with Art Nouveau villas and a mock-Moorish castle.

Since the Lido cannot compete with the historical riches of the rest of Venice, it generally remains the preserve of residents and visitors staying on the island. Although most day-

Death in Venice

Death and Venice go together, with the lagoon a familiar backdrop to modern murder mysteries. The city's taste for the macabre is partly a romanticised notion fed by visions of sinister alleys, the inkiness of a lagoon night or a *cortège* of mourning gondolas gliding across the water. However, Venetian history does provide tales of murdered Doges and deadly plots nipped in the bud by the secret police.

And the most celebrated work of literature set in Venice, Thomas Mann's novella *Death in Venice*, does little to dispel the myth. The book follows the decline of the writer Gustav von Aschenbach – a man who believes that art is produced only in 'defiant despite' of corrupting passions and physical weakness. On a reluctant break from work, Aschenbach finds himself in Venice, which Mann depicts as a place of decadence and spiritual dislocation. Aschenbach's obsession with a beautiful Polish boy staying at his hotel (the Lido's Hotel des Bains) has dire consequences, as he becomes a slave to his passions, ignoring a cholera epidemic that the corrupt Venetian authorities try to conceal.

Beach houses at the Lido

trippers stray no further than the smart hotels and the beaches where the poets Byron and Shelley once raced on horseback, the Lido offers subtle pleasures for those willing to look, from belle époque architecture to a delightful cycle ride along the sea walls to Malamocco.

The ferries from San Marco deposit visitors among the traffic at the edge of the shopping district. Close to the jetties stands the 16th-century church of **Santa Maria Elisabetta**; behind is the main street, Gran Viale Santa Maria Elisabetta, which cuts across the island from the lagoon shore to the Adriatic. At the far end of the Viale lies the **Lungomare**, the seafront promenade and the focus of the summer evening *passeggiata* (promenade). Beyond are the best Adriatic beaches, private pockets of sand bedecked with colourful cabins.

The Lido is home to several of the city's most elegant hotels, including the palatial **Hotel des Bains**, which helped to inspire Thomas Mann's *Death in Venice (see box opposite).*

WHAT TO DO

ENTERTAINMENT

For visitors in search of cultural entertainment Venice can't be faulted, with year-round classical concerts, opera, theatre, art exhibitions and festivals to suit all tastes. Those looking for bars and clubs fare less well, due to a large degree to the fact that the average age in Venice is 45. For details of what's on when, ask for a copy of the *Venice Magazine* (www.venicemagazine.it/Eindex.htm) from the tourist office – it comes with a useful 'Events and Shows' booklet. The website www.meetingvenice.it also has information on performances and events.

The Performance Arts

Classical music is everywhere. The most popular venues for concerts, from organ recitals to choral works, are Venice's many churches, especially San Bartolomeo, Santo Stefano, the Frari, San Vidal and the Salute; the Scuole (charitable confraternities) are also important venues for music of this kind. To the chagrin of the locals, there tends to be a preponderance of groups specialising in Venice's very own Antonio Vivaldi, although most give highly accomplished performances. The chamber group Interpreti Veneziani (www.interpretiveneziani.com) is a good name to look for. A number of ensembles, including I Musici Veneziani (www.imusiciveneziani.com) and Orchestra di Venezia (www.veneziaclassic.it), a Baroque chamber orchestra, perform in costume.

Opera in Venice has a rather tragic history – the city's main opera house, **La Fenice** (The Phoenix), on Campo San

Traditional Venetian masks

Fantin, once dubbed 'the prettiest theatre in Europe', was badly damaged by fire in 1996 – its third fire since its construction in 1774. It reopened in 2004 with a triumphant performance of Verdi's *La Traviata*. The opera season runs from November until May. For information on performances and tickets phone the HelloVenezia call centre on 041-2424 or visit www.teatrolafenice.it.

Another attractive venue for opera is the **Teatro Malibran** (Cannaregio 5873; tel: 041-786 601), a tiny jewel of a theatre that reopened in 2001 after 10 years of restoration. Dating from 1678, when it was known as Il Teatro di San Giovanni Grisostomo, the building was renamed in the 19th century when it was dedicated to a celebrated diva, Maria Malibran.

Opera fans may also be interested in the summer programme at the **Arena** in nearby Verona.

For drama, try the **Teatro Goldoni** (San Marco 4650; tel: 041-240 2011), which offers a year-round programme of plays performed by Italian and international companies, some with translations.

Nightlife

With Venice's elderly resident population and large number of day-trippers, nightlife is somewhat restrained – focused on piano bars, the historic cafés around San Marco and chic hotel bars. In recent years, however, the nightlife scene has been livened up with a number of hip late-night lounge bars. For that authentic Venetian experience, traditional bars known as *bacari (see box on page 102)* are certainly worth a visit.

Nightlife listings can be found in *Un Ospite di Venezia*, available from a few top hotels *(see page 122)*, and in a booklet produced by Rolling Venice *(see page 115)*.

Just west of Piazza San Marco, **Bacaro Lounge** in Salizzada San Moisè is a hip cocktail bar with jazz music and a restaurant. **Bistrot de Venise** on Calle dei Fabbri, north of Piazza San Marco, is a rare eatery that stays open very late and organises concerts and poetry recitals on certain nights.

If you're prepared to venture away from Piazza San Marco, you'll be rewarded with a scattering of late-night bars, mostly frequented by students and young Venetians. Dorsoduro, with its student district, is home to the best nightspots, including **Piccolo Mondo**, an off-beat disco with a mixed clientele just west of the Accademia, and the lively late-night bars and cafés in Campo Santa Margherita. **Margaret DuChamp** is a fashionable bar on the square, and **Orange** is a contemporary lounge bar with an in-house DJ.

Venice's municipal **Casinò** (tel: 041-529 7111; www.casino venezia.it) is in the Palazzo Vendramin-Calergi on the Grand Canal. Games, including roulette, chemin de fer, poker and blackjack, are played until the early hours. Valid ID is essen-

Drinks at the bar

tial for admittance to the gambling rooms, as are jackets for men (available to hire). Visitors must be over 18.

Film Festival

The **Venice Film Festival** (Mostra Internazionale d'Arte Cinematografica) is a major event on the international cinema circuit, lasting for 10 days in late August/early September. At this balmy time of the year, the city welcomes the stars, who can be seen parading along the seafront or sipping Bellinis on the grand terrace of the Excelsior Hotel, where the first film festival (reputedly also the world's first, predating Cannes by 14 years) opened in 1932. Founded as a showcase for Fascist Italy, the festival's success belies its unpromising origins.

It's usually difficult for visitors outside the film and press industries to attend the festival, but for information, check www.labiennale.org. If you want to try your luck, the action is centred around the Lido by day and San Marco by night.

Carnevale

The black cloak, tricorn hat, white mask and other rather sinister garb identified with Venice's Carnevale date back to the 18th century when the *commedia dell'arte* was in vogue. In the final century of the decadent, drifting Republic, Carnevale was extended to six months, and Venetians wore these costumes from December to June. Under this guise of anonymity, commoner and aristocrat were interchangeable, husbands and wives could pursue amours unchallenged, and all sorts of misdemeanors could be committed. Things got so out of hand that Carnevale was eventually banned.

Today's Carnevale, revived only in 1979 and held in February/March, is more restrained. Nonetheless, this is one time of year that the city really comes to life, with street parties, masked balls, pageants, special events and visitors from all over Europe.

Smart shops located near Piazza San Marco

SHOPPING

One of the most satisfying aspects of shopping in Venice is separating the treasure-house from the tourist trap. As a general rule, the high-end shops (jewellery, glassware, leather) are located around **Piazza San Marco**. However, this area is also home to a proliferation of tacky tourist shops, offering overpriced souvenirs. For less tourist-orientated purchases, head for the **Strada Nuova**, which runs behind the Ca' d'Oro towards the railway station. The odd bargain can be found in artisans' workshops in the **Dorsoduro** behind the Zattere and on the **Giudecca**, while the artisans' shops on the **Frezzeria** behind Piazza San Marco offer more affordable prices.

For fashion, the shopping street of **Mercerie** (described in 1645 by John Evelyn as 'the most delicious streete in the world') has quality boutiques, which become increasingly affordable the further away from Piazza San Marco you head.

Glassware

Contemporary Venetian glassware poses a problem of quality and price, so hunt carefully. The factories on **Murano** rarely offer better prices than shops in mainland Venice, but they will give free demonstrations and transport to the island. When choosing gifts to be shipped, bypass the extremely fragile items and always ask for handling and insurance rates before you buy, as they may double the price. For more information, visit www.muranoglass.com.

Lace

The small lace museum on **Burano** is the best place to see samples of exquisite handcrafted laceware; upstairs you can sometimes find Buranese women busily knotting away in the old tradition. The real thing is exorbitantly priced, with many lesser-quality, machine-made pieces from the Far East being

Mask-maker's workshop in Castello district

passed off as locally hand-made. If you don't have time to visit Burano, you can buy modern reproductions and interpretations of traditional patterns around San Marco.

Marbled Paper

Venice is also famed for its marbled paper, made by a process where a special mixture is spread on the paper, then wavy patterns, like peacock's feathers, are created by teasing a comb through the mixture. Paper of this

Murano glass

kind used to be popular for binding books and pamphlets and as a background for documents, thus providing protection against forgery. Today, it is used mainly to make photograph albums, writing cases, greeting cards and notebooks.

SPORTS

Venice itself offers few leisure facilities for the sporty visitor. At the end of each October, the city hosts a world-class **marathon** that attracts more than 6,000 runners from across the world. If you want to participate, contact your local running club for details or visit www.venicemarathon.it.

A more relaxed option is a trip to the Lido, where from June to September most of the private beaches of the large hotels offer a variety of water sports, including **windsurfing**, **water-skiing**, **canoeing** and dinghy and catamaran **sailing**. However, swimming is not always permitted on the Lido's beaches due to pollution problems. The Lido also has an 18-

hole **golf** course at Alberoni-Lido (open all year round, clubs for hire) and, in summer, **tennis** courts open to the public.

Knowledge of the lagoon's channels is necessary for safe boating, so motorboats are not rented out to tourists. However, if you belong to a **rowing** club at home and can produce proof of membership, one of the local rowing clubs may let you join their ranks. Contact the Società Cannottieri Bucintoro, Zattere ai Saloni, Dorsoduro (tel: 041-520 5630; www.bucintoro.org).

CHILDREN'S VENICE

The waterways of Venice never fail to impress the young at heart, making a gondola ride *(see page 58)* a good choice for parents in search of family entertainment. However, if the inflated cost of a gondola brings tears to your eyes, simply take the kids on a *vaporetto* – Venice's waterbuses offer the distinct advantage that children under 4 years of age travel free, and there are reduced fares for families. Excursions to the Lido, where there are beaches, water rides and pedalos, are always popular with children in summer.

Delicious *gelato*

Other child-friendly options include: watching the glass-blowers at **Murano** *(see page 80)*; visiting the **Museo Storico Navale** *(see page 47)*, with its fascinating array of model and life-size ships; climbing up the **Campanile di San Marco** *(see page 32)*. Finally, consider visiting in July during the **Festa del Redentore** with its fabulous fireworks *(see opposite)*.

Festivals and Events

1 Jan *Capodanno* (New Year's Day). Celebrations on the beach.

Feb–Mar *Carnevale* (Carnival). Ten-day, pre-Lenten extravaganza with masked balls, processions, pantomime and music *(see page 92)*. The high point comes on Shrove Tuesday with a masked ball in Piazza San Marco, after which the effigy of Carnival is burned in the square.

25 Apr *Festa di San Marco* (St Mark's Day). Ceremonial Mass in the Basilica, when rosebuds *(bocolo)* are given as love tokens. A gondola race is also held between Sant'Elena and the Punta della Dogana, followed by a traditional meal of *risi e bisi* ('rice and peas'), actually a kind of soup.

Sunday after Ascension *La Sensa*, celebrating Venice's 'marriage with the sea'. Re-enacts trips made to the Lido by the doges, who cast rings into the water to symbolise the union of the Republic and the sea.

Two Sundays after Ascension *La Vogalonga* (literally: 'long row'). Hundreds of rowing boats follow a 32-km (20-mile) course from the Basino di San Marco to Burano and then San Francesco del Deserto.

June–Nov *Biennale Arte* (odd years only). Art exhibition held in the Arsenale and Giardini Pubblici *(see page 46)*. *Biennale Architettura* (even years only). Architecture exhibition in the same spaces.

July, third Sunday *Festa del Redentore* (Festival of the Redeemer). A sweeping bridge of boats bedecked in finery and glowing with lights stretches across the Giudecca canal to Il Redentore church. There is a spectacular firework display on the eve of the feast day.

Aug For 10 days, from late August, Venice hosts its International Film Festival *(see page 92)* at the Lido by day, San Marco by night.

15 Aug *Ferragosto* (Assumption). Concerts on Torcello.

Sept, first Sunday *La Regata Storica* (Historical Regatta) The finest regatta of the year, which begins with a procession up the Grand Canal led by costumed Venetians, followed by gondola races.

Nov–May Opera season at La Fenice.

21 November *Festa della Salute*. Processions to the candlelit Santa Maria della Salute, commemorating the city's deliverance from the plague of 1630.

EATING OUT

Most Venetians have traditional attitudes toward food, and the city's restaurants reflect this, focussing on Venetian and Italian dishes. There is little in the way of international cuisine, except a few Italian-influenced Chinese restaurants and a few attempts at French cuisine in the more expensive hotels. Venetian food is heavily influenced by the bounty of the lagoon, with fresh fish, clams, shrimps, calamari, *seppie* (cuttlefish) and octopus all featuring heavily; duck and game birds, which inhabit the marshy islands, are also popular.

WHERE TO EAT

The San Marco area is awash with overpriced tourist-traps that no Venetian would consider frequenting. Most of the city's best restaurants are in the Dorsoduro, San Polo and Santa Croce neighbourhoods, just across the Grand Canal from San Marco. In theory, the word *ristorante* usually indicates a large, elaborate establishment, whereas a *trattoria* is a cosy, perhaps family-run, place and an *osteria* has a rustic atmosphere. Yet in Venice, as elsewhere in Italy, the distinction is often blurred beyond all recognition. Price should not be taken as an indication of quality – an expensive restaurant may offer a superb meal with service to match, but you will pay for the location. That said, there are still some fabulous top-notch restaurants here for those wishing to push the boat out.

Around San Marco, many restaurants offer a *menù turistico*, a fixed-price set menu. Although this may appear to be cheaper than eating *à la carte*, portions will invariably be smaller and the choice limited. If you are on a budget try a *bacaro* (traditional wine bar; *see page 102*), which often serve reasonably priced meals as well as substantial snacks.

Italian restaurants have to display the menu with prices in the window or just inside the door, so you will have an idea of what's offered before you take the plunge. The bill usually includes service *(servizio)* of between 10 and 15 percent, but ask if you're not sure. It's normal to round the bill up slightly in addition to this.

Meal times are from noon to 2.30 or 3pm, and from around 7.30 to 10pm. Nearly all restaurants close at least one day per week and many also shut during part of late July, August, January and February.

Canal-side dining, Dorsoduro

VENETIAN CUISINE

Most Venetians start the day with *piccola colazione* – a coffee (a strong dark *espresso* or a foaming milky cappuccino) and bread roll or croissant *(cornetto)*; the best place for this is a *caffè*. Remember that in a bar what you consume will cost twice as much if you eat it sitting at a table than standing at the bar. If you're breakfasting in a hotel, the larger chains usually serve an English- or American-style buffet.

For a quick snack at lunchtime, choose a *tavola calda*, a stand-up bar serving a variety of hot and cold dishes to take away or eat on the spot. For a larger meal, at both lunch *(pranzo)* and dinner *(cena)* there is generally a choice of four

A floating market stall

courses: *antipasti* (starters or appetisers); *primo piatto* (first course); *secondo piatto* (main course) with *contorni* (vegetable or salad accompaniments) and *dolce* (dessert). Don't worry if you're just looking for a light bite – you certainly won't be expected to order all four courses.

Appetisers

Any *trattoria* worth its olive oil will offer a good selection of *antipasti*, either vegetarian, fish-based or meaty. A popular vegetarian choice is *carciofi* (artichokes), while those with fish include: *sarde in saor* (marinated sardines and onions, with pine kernels and raisins); *frutti di mare* (seafood), prawns, baby octopus, mussels and squid in a lemon dressing; and *vongole*, *caparozzoli* (both types of clam) or *cozze* (mussels), in a white-wine sauce. Meaty *antipasti* include *carpaccio*, thin slices of raw beef dressed with olive oil; *prosciutto crudo con melone* (ham with melon), sometimes offered with figs *(fichi)*; and *affettati* or spicy *salsicce* (charcuterie and salami-style sausage).

First Course

The *primo piatto* is usually pasta, risotto or soup. This far north, pasta often takes second place to rice, and risotto is often recognised as *the* classic Venetian dish. Its constituents are usually fresh vegetables or seafood. Venice's most famous pasta dish is *bigoli in salsa* (noodles in an anchovy or tuna sauce). *Zuppa di pesce* (a stew-like fish soup) is usually a good choice. *Pasta e fagioli* is a delicious thick pasta-and-white-bean soup.

Main Course

Seafood dominates the *secondo piatto*, and if you are lucky it will be the catch of the day. *Fritto misto* (mixed fried fish) or the more expensive *grigliata mista* (grilled fish) are two favourite dishes. Fish that feature heavily on menus here include *coda di rospo* (monkfish), *orata* (gilt-head bream), *branzino/spigola* (sea-bass), *San Pietro* (John Dory) and *sogliola* (sole). Local seafood favourites are *granceola* (spidercrab served in its own shell), *anguilla alla veneziana* (eel cooked in a sauce made with lemon, oil and tuna) and *seppie al nero* (cuttlefish in its own ink) traditionally served with *polenta*.

Meat dishes are rarely inspiring but one of the best bets is the Venetian favourite *fegato alla veneziana* (calf's liver with onions), served with polenta. *Vitello tonnato* (thin slices of cold veal fillet in tuna sauce) is also a good dish to try.

Rucola (rocket) and *radicchio* (a type of chicory from Treviso) are popular components of **salads**, while assorted grilled **vegetables** are common side dishes.

Desserts and Cheese

The dessert choice is often limited to around half a dozen items, including *gelato* (ice-cream) and *tiramisù* (literally 'pick me up'), a chilled coffee-flavoured, trifle-like confection. *Panna cotta* ('cooked cream') has a similar texture to crème caramel, but a lighter taste. A typical Venetian custom is to serve *vino dolce con biscotti*, a glass of dessert wine with sweet biscuits.

Cheese. Strong *gorgonzola* is popular, often served with *parmigiano* or *grana* (both parmesan). Among the delicacies of the Veneto province is a savoury, tangy cow's milk cheese named after the mountain town of Asiago.

Snacks

The city's many bars and cafés offer stacks of assorted *tramezzini* (white bread sandwiches, which can be heavy on the mayonnaise) and *panini* (filled rolls). For tapas-style snacks, try a *bacaro (see box below)*.

Cichetti and Ombre

If you want to eat economically and try as many local delicacies as possible, look out for *bacari*, or tradional wine bars; these have counters of *cichetti* (plates of snacks, similar to *tapas*), from herbed shelled lobster claws drizzled with olive oil, to smoky grilled *calamari* and *pizzette* (tiny pizzas). At most bars, cafés, and *bacari*, there is no seating – everyone simply stands and nibbles the snacks with a glass of house wine in hand – even if there is seating, remember that food costs up to twice as much if you sit down, so most Venetians stand at the bar anyway.

Un ombrà (literally, 'shade') is the Venetian term for house wine, a phrase that comes from the fact that the locals 'step into the shade' when they break for a glass of wine. *Ombra di rosso* is the house red, *ombra di bianco* the house white.

Venice's most famous wine bar is Cantina do Mori on Calle do Mori near the Rialto Bridge. Founded in 1462, it's a dark place, crammed with brass pots. It serves fabulous *cichetti* and a variety of Veneto wines.

A selection of tasty *cichetti*

WHAT TO DRINK

Most restaurants offer the open wine of the house, red or white, in quarter-, half- or 1-litre carafes, as well as a good selection of bottled vintages. Many Veneto wines, including Soave, Valpolicella and Bardolino, will probably be familiar, thanks to their export success. The local wine region of Friuli supplies good Pinot Grigio, as well as palatable house wines *(vini della casa)*. To widen your knowledge of the local wines, look out for an *enoteca*, a combination of bar and wine retailer.

Two sparkling drinks, consumed in cafés all over town, are Prosecco, a great sparkling white wine, and *spritz*, a combination of Campari, white wine and sparkling mineral water. Venice's other drink of note is the bellini, an ambrosial concoction of Prosecco and fresh peach juice. It was invented by Signor Cipriani, the father of the current proprietor of

Dining al fresco on the Fondamenta San Lorenzo in Castello

Harry's Bar *(see page 106)*, the city's most famous (and most expensive) restaurant and night spot.

Bitters such as Campari and Punt e Mes are refreshing appetisers with soda and lemon. For after-dinner drinks, the options range from throat-warming *vecchia romagna* brandy, to sweet *strega*, almond-flavoured *amaretto*, aniseed-tasting *sambuca* and fiery *grappa* – there is no specifically Venetian *digestif*. For beer-drinkers, Nastro Azzuro is a national favourite; this brew, which is not as strong as most north European brands, is usually served refreshingly ice cold.

Non-alcoholic drinks range from wonderfully potent coffees and frothy hot chocolate to refreshing iced tea. Mineral water *(acqua minerale)* is a normal accompaniment to a meal – for sparkling, ask for *gasata*; still is *naturale*. Tap water in Venice is safe to drink unless marked *acqua non potabile*. The water from the many drinking fountains around the city is also perfectly safe.

TO HELP YOU ORDER

Waiter/waitress	**Cameriere/cameriera**		
Do you have a set menu?	**Avete un menù a prezzo fisso?**		
I'd like a/an/some ...	**Vorrei ...**		
beer	**una birra**	pepper	**del pepe**
bread	**del pane**	potatoes	**delle patate**
butter	**del burro**	salad	**un'insalata**
coffee	**un caffè**	salt	**del sale**
cream	**della panna**	soup	**una minestra**
fish	**del pesce**	sugar	**dello zucchero**
fruit	**della frutta**	tea	**un tè**
ice-cream	**un gelato**	water	**dell'acqua**
meat	**della carne**	(mineral)	**(minerale)**
milk	**del latte**	wine	**del vino**

MENU READER

aglio	garlic	**manzo**	beef
agnello	lamb	**mela**	apple
albicocche	apricots	**melanzane**	aubergine
aragosta	lobster	**merluzzo**	cod
arancia	orange	**ostriche**	oysters
bistecca	beefsteak	**pesca**	peach
calamari	squid	**pollo**	chicken
carciofi	artichokes	**pomodori**	tomatoes
cipolle	onions	**prosciutto**	ham
crostacei	shellfish	**rognoni**	kidneys
fegato	liver	**tacchino**	turkey
fichi	figs	**tonno**	tuna
formaggio	cheese	**uovo**	egg
frutti di mare	seafood	**uva**	grapes
funghi	mushrooms	**verdure**	vegetables
lamponi	raspberries	**vitello**	veal
maiale	pork	**vongole**	clams

PLACES TO EAT

We have used the following symbols to give an idea of the price for a three-course meal for one, including wine, cover and service:

€€€€ over 75 euros   €€ 30–50 euros
€€€ 50–75 euros   € below 30 euros

SAN MARCO

Bistrot de Venise €€ *Calle dei Fabbri, San Marco 4685, tel: 041-523 6651, www.bistrotdevenise.com.* Venetians and visitors alike come for salads at lunch and tried-and-tested recipes at night. A good place for night owls, this bistro north of Piazza San Marco stays open until midnight; occasional live music. ACTV: Rialto.

Da Ivo €€€€ *Ramo dei Fuseri, San Marco 1809, tel: 041-528 5004, www.ristorantedaivo.com.* Both Venetian and Tuscan cuisines are served at this upmarket restaurant northwest of Piazza San Marco. Risotto with cuttlefish ink heads the menu, while Florentine specialities include chicken and T-bone steak. However, the main pull is the atmospheric, intimate dining room. Closed Sun and Jan 6–31. ACTV: Vallaresso.

Harry's Bar €€€€ *Calle Vallaresso, San Marco 1323, tel: 041-528 5777, www.cipriani.com.* This legendary hotspot near the Vallaresso landing stage has prices to make you weep but on a good day it does heavenly food – *carpaccio* (thin slices of raw beef) was invented here. The *bellini* (prosecco and fresh white peach juice) is also an invention of Harry's, though best avoided out of peach season. It's more stylish to dine downstairs at the bar, as Hemingway did, rather than upstairs. ACTV: Vallaresso.

La Cusina €€€€ *Hotel Westin Europa e Regina, off Calle Larga XXII Marzo, San Marco 2159, tel: 041-240 0001.* A combination of the most dramatic terrace on the Grand Canal and beautifully presented Venetian *haute cuisine* make this a good choice for that special romantic dinner. ACTV: Vallaresso.

Osteria Ai Assassini €€ *Rio Terrà degli Assassini, San Marco 3695, tel: 041-528 7986, www.osteriaaiassassini.it.* Lively tavern-like place with great soups near the Palazzo Contarini del Bovolo. Baked fish and seafood dishes are the best choices here; *cappe sante al pomodoro* (scallops with tomato) come highly recommended. Closed Sun. ACTV: Sant' Angelo.

Rosticceria San Bartolomeo € *Calle della Bissa, San Marco 5424, tel: 041-522 3569.* East of the Rialto Bridge this place displays delicious food, which is served at a fast counter on the ground floor or, for slightly more money, in a restaurant section upstairs. It tends to be packed except for off-peak hours. Takeaways available. ACTV: Rialto.

CASTELLO

Al Covo €€€€ *Campiello della Pescheria (just off the Riva degli Schiavoni), Castello 3968, tel: 041-522 3812, www.ristorealcovo.com.* This relaxed, cosy restaurant created by chef Cesare Benelli and his Texan wife, Diane, has a worldwide reputation for excellent quality fresh seafood innovatively prepared according to Venetian traditions. During the autumn, duck and game birds are added to the menu. Closed Wed and Thurs. ACTV: San Zaccaria.

Alla Rivetta €€ *Ponte San Provolo, west of Campo San Zaccaria, Castello 4625, tel: 041-528 7302.* The emphasis in this lively restaurant is on fish dishes, especially with fish-and-pasta combinations, such as gnocchi stuffed with crab. The *tiramisù* and *cichetti* are also excellent. Closed Mon. ACTV: San Zaccaria.

Alle Testiere €€–€€€ *Calle del Mondo Novo, Castello 5801, tel: 041-522 7220.* A tiny place off Campo Santa Maria della Formosa with a changing daily menu and inventive twists on traditional Venetian cuisine. Great wine list. Reservations essential. Closed Sun and Mon. ACTV: Rialto.

Corte Sconta €€€–€€€€ *Calle del Pestrin, Castello 3886, tel: 041-522 7024.* This hard-to-find rustic restaurant west of the Arsenale has a garden courtyard and one of the best menus in town, with superb *antipasti* and seafood and outstanding house wine. Closed Sun, Mon, Jan and mid-July to mid-Aug. ACTV: Arsenale.

Mascareta €€ *Calle Lunga Santa Maria Formosa, Castello 5183, tel: 041-523 0744.* A bustling casual place near Campo Santa Maria della Formosa, with a young clientele, Mascareta is great for wine and *cichetti* (snacks). ACTV: Rialto.

Metropole Hotel €€€€ *Riva degli Schiavoni, Castello 4149, tel: 041-520 5044.* This hotel on the waterfront has an elegant, Michelin-starred restaurant, which specialises in traditional Venetian cuisine. Garden dining in summer. Reservations necessary. ACTV: San Zaccaria.

Osteria di Santa Marina €€€€ *Campo Santa Marina, Castello 5911, tel: 041-528 5239.* Traditional and delightful restaurant east of the Rialto Bridge with tables on the square in summer. Specialises in creative seafood cuisine based on Venetian classics. Closed Sun and Mon. ACTV: Rialto.

Trattoria da Remigio €€€ *Salizzada dei Greci, Castello 3416, tel: 041-523 0089.* A simple indoor trattoria north of La Pieta that is popular with the locals. Try the gnocchi or one of the many fish specials. Closed Mon evening and Tue. ACTV: San Zaccaria.

DORSODURO

Ai Gondolieri €€€€ *Fondamenta Zorzi Bragadini, Dorsoduro 36, tel: 041-528 6396, www.aigondolieri.com.* South of the Guggenheim, this canalside restaurant attracts connoisseurs for some of the best meat and vegetables in Venice, prepared *nouvelle-cuisine* style. Try the stuffed courgettes. Note that they don't do fish. Closed Tue. ACTV: Accademia.

Collezione Peggy Guggenheim Café €–€€ *Dorsoduro 701, tel: 041-522 8688.* With a menu of salads, soups, pasta and fish created by nearby Ai Gondolieri's chef, this is a gem if you're visiting the museum. Desserts are fabulous. Open 10am–6pm; closed Tue. ACTV: Accademia or Salute.

La Bitta €€ *Calle Lunga San Barnaba, Dorsoduro 2753A, tel: 041-523 0531*. Informal little restaurant near Campo San Barnaba which serves almost entirely meat. Good value and popular with the locals. Closed Sun. ACTV: Ca' Rezzonico.

La Furatola €€€–€€€€ *Calle Lunga San Barnaba 2870A, tel: 041-520 8594*. A cosy place west of Campo San Barnaba that is famous for its fresh fish. The ample portions of pasta are often big enough to share. Fabulous desserts. Closed Mon lunch, Wed, Thurs and Aug. ACTV: Ca' Rezzonico.

L'Avogaria €€–€€€ *Calle dell'Avogaria, Dorsoduro 1629, tel: 041-296 0491, www.avogaria.com*. Mouth-watering specialities from Puglia served in a stylish designer eatery near San Sebastiano at the far west of the Dorsoduro region. Closed Tue. ACTV: San Basilio.

Riviera €€€ *Zattere, Dorsoduro 1473, tel: 041-522 7621, www.ristoranteriviera.it*. With outdoor seating overlooking the Giudecca Canal at the western end of the Zattere, the stylish Riviera is famous for exquisite homemade pasta and very fresh fish and seafood. Closed Mon all day and lunch on Tue. ACTV: San Basilio.

Taverna San Trovaso €–€€ *Fondamenta Priuli, Dorsoduro 1016, tel: 041-520 3703, www.tavernasantrovaso.it*. This friendly pizzeria/trattoria just west of the Accademia gallery is popular with the locals, especially with families. Book a table downstairs in the brick-vaulted room. Portions are large, even on the good-value *menù turistico*. Closed Mon. ACTV: Accademia.

SAN POLO AND SANTA CROCE

Alla Madonna €–€€€ *Calle della Madonna (west of the Rialto Bridge), San Polo 594, tel: 041-522 3824, www.ristorantealla madonna.com*. Venice's most famous medium-priced fish restaurant is a maze of beamed and stuccoed rooms and it caters for a variety of tastes – visitors, locals, students and business people alike congregate here. Reservations only for parties of eight or more. Closed Wed. ACTV: Rialto.

Alla Zucca €€ *Ponte del Megio, off Campo San Giacomo dell'* *Orio, Santa Croce 1762, tel: 041-524 1570, www.lazucca.it.* This small, modern place offers a pleasant, relaxed atmosphere. The menu is strong on pasta and inventive vegetable dishes but there are also meat dishes and excellent desserts. Dine outside beside a small canal in summer. Closed Sun. ACTV: San Stae.

Antica Trattoria Poste Vecchie €€€ *Pescaria, San Polo 1608, tel: 041-721 822.* The city's oldest restaurant, near the fish market, is a warren of tiny atmospheric rooms, some dating from the 16th century. Fish dominates the menu. Closed Tue. ACTV: Rialto.

Naranzaria €€ *Erbaria, San Polo 130, tel: 041-724 1035, www. naranzaria.it.* Fashionable *osteria* overlooking the Grand Canal. The focus is on raw food prepared with ingredients fresh from the neighbouring Rialto markets. Try the tuna and salmon *maki*, raw prawns with spicy seaweed or *carpaccio* of swordfish. Also serves hot cuisine and meat dishes.

Osteria Da Fiore €€€€ *Calle del Scaleter, (north of Campo di* *San Polo), San Polo 2002, tel: 041-721 308, www.dafiore.net.* Simplicity, top-quality food and the inimitable skills of chef Maria Martin have gained this elegant, rather formal little place rave reviews from international food critics and a Michelin star. Closed Sun, Mon and Aug. ACTV: San Stae.

Pizzeria ae Oche € *Calle del Tintor (off Campo San Giacomo* *dell'Orio), Santa Croce 1552, tel: 041-524 1161, www.aeoche.* *com.* This informal place offers an incredible range of excellent pizzas in unpretentious surroundings – hence the frequent queues. Closed Mon. ACTV: San Stae.

CANNAREGIO

Al Fontego dei Pescaori €€–€€€ *Calle Priuli, Cannaregio 3726, tel: 041-520 0538, www.alfontego.com.* The owner of this restaurant north of the Ca' d'Oro is president of the Rialto fish market and has his own stall, so you can be guaranteed the freshest fish and seafood. Closed Mon. ACTV: Ca' d'Oro.

Brek € *Lista di Spagna, Cannaregio 124, www.brek.it.* Excellent value self-service chain offering pasta, pizza, freshly made hot dishes, salads and fresh fruit. ACTV: Ferrovia.

Fiaschetteria Toscana €€€ *Salizzada San Giovanni Crisostomo (northeast of the Rialto Bridge), Cannaregio 5719, tel: 041-528 5281, www.fiaschetteriatoscana.it.* Despite its name, Venetian cuisine prevails in this gracious but often crowded family-run restaurant with a garden. Top choices include the excellent fish selection – notably scallops with almonds, cuttlefish or *schie* (tiny shrimps) with polenta – liver *alla veneziana* and great desserts. Closed Tue and lunch on Wed; and July. ACTV: Rialto.

GIUDECCA

Harry's Dolci €€€–€€€€ *Fondamenta San Biagio, Giudecca 773 (near Sant'Eufemia landing stage), tel: 041-522 4844.* Shares its management and gourmet menu with Harry's Bar *(see page 106)*, but slightly less expensive and has sweeping views of Venice across the Giudecca Canal. It's also popular for the divine desserts. Closed Tue; Nov–mid-Mar. ACTV: Palanca.

THE ISLANDS

Ai Pescatori €€–€€€ *Piazza Galuppi, 371 Burano, tel: 041-730 650.* The excellent, family-owned Ai Pescatori is supplied with fresh fish by the island's fishermen. Great *moleche fritte* or *anguilla alla buranese*. Closed Wed.

Busa alla Torre €€–€€€ *Campo Santo Stefano, Murano, tel: 041-739 662.* Good seafood served at fabulous tables beside the water in the southeast part of the island. Packed on weekends. Lunch only.

Locanda Cipriani €€€€ *Piazza Santa Fosca 29, Torcello, tel: 041-730 150.* Idyllic, rustic spot near the basilica renowned for its cuisine. Simple, classic dishes such as *carpaccio cipriani*, fish grills and *risotto alla Torcellano*, with lagoon vegetables and herbs. Reservations essential. Closed Tue; and Jan.

A–Z TRAVEL TIPS

A Summary of Practical Information

A

ACCOMMODATION (For RECOMMENDED HOTELS, see page 131)

Venice is home to some of Europe's finest **hotels** as well as basic dormitories. Like the city, most of the accommodation is old and characterful. Many of the city's hotels *(alberghi)* are housed in old palaces. When making reservations, ask for a room with a view, and, when checking in, ask to see a number of different rooms, as they can vary greatly in quality. If your budget allows, go for a top-level room with a private roof deck. In budget hotels, always check if there is air-conditioning, and, if there is, whether there is an extra charge for it.

Advance booking is essential during peak periods, when some hotels are booked up months in advance: at Carnival *(see page 92)*, April to June, September and October, around Christmas and New Year, and weekends year-round. In the chill of winter prices can drop by as much as 50 percent. It can also be easier and more affordable to get a room during the sweltering mid-summer period (July and August), when the city's tourism is largely made up of day-trippers. Many Lido hotels are only open from April to October.

For a list of hotels contact the tourist office (www.turismovenezia.it, *see pages 127–8*). You can also book online at the Hoteliers' Association website (www.veneziasi.it), but for the best rates book directly with the hotel.

In recent years the city has seen a huge increase in the number of **guesthouses**. These usually offer better value than hotels as well as the opportunity to get to know the Venetian owners.

Do you have any vacancies?	**Avete camere libere?**
I'd like a single/double room	**Vorrei una camera singola/ matrimoniale**
with (without) bath/shower	**con (senza) bagno/doccia**
What's the rate per night?	**Qual è il prezzo per una notte?**

Self-catering **apartments**, often within beautiful palazzi, are worth considering, particularly for families. Contact Venetian Apartments (www.venice-rentals.com) for a wide selection.

AIRPORTS (Aeroporti)

Venice Marco Polo (VCE; tel: 041-260 9260; www.veniceairport.it) is Venice's main airport, located 13km (8 miles) north of the city.

Public buses (ACTV, €1) run from the airport to the terminus at Piazzale Roma every half-hour in summer and about once an hour in winter; **airport buses** (ATVO, €3) have a similar timetable. Both take around 30 minutes to reach Piazzale Roma. Once at Piazzale Roma (just across the Grand Canal from the train station), board a *vaporetto* (€6.50; No. 1 stops at all stages along the Grand Canal; No. 2 is a faster service). A land **taxi** from the airport to Piazzale Roma costs around €40.

For water transport from Marco Polo airport you have to walk about 500m from the new terminal to the small dock area. Trollies and porters are both available. The Alilaguna **water launches** (www.alilaguna.it) provide a year-round direct service between Marco Polo airport and central Venice. Tickets (€13 per person) can be purchased at the Alilaguna pier, or on board for €14. The red and blue lines take around 80 minutes to reach San Marco via Murano and the Lido, then go on to Zattere (Dorsoduro). The orange line takes 60 minutes to the Rialto via the railway station. The gold line takes 60 minutes to San Marco but costs €25.

Private **water taxis** *(taxi acquei)* are the fastest means to reach the centre (30 mins) but are very expensive at approximately €135 for four people and luggage, so be careful not to confuse them with the Alilaguna craft. However, they will take you right up to your hotel if it has a water entrance, or drop you off as close as possible.

Treviso (TSF; tel: 042-231 5111; www.trevisoairport.it) is a small airport 30km (20 miles) north of Venice, used mainly by charter companies and low-cost airlines, who often, confusingly, call it

'Venice airport'. ATVO's Eurobus runs between Treviso airport and Piazzale Roma (1hr 10 mins), connecting with most flights.

Where's the boat/bus for…?	**Dove si prende il vaporetto/ l'autobus per…?**
I want a ticket to…	**Desidero uno biglietto per…**
Could you please take these bags to the bus/train/taxi	**Mi porti queste valige fino all'autobus/al treno/al taxi, per favore**
What time does the train/bus leave for the city centre?	**A che ora parte il treno/ pullman per il centro?**

B

BUDGETING FOR YOUR TRIP

Discount passes. Venice Connected (www.veniceconnected.com) is a new multifunctional pass whereby you choose from transport, sightseeing and leisure options and pay accordingly. To get the cheapest rates you should book online at least 15 days in advance. Prices also vary according to the time of year.

Those aged between 14 and 29 can buy a **Rolling Venice** card at any tourist office or the ACTV office in Piazzale Roma. The card costs €4 and provides discounts on 25 museums and galleries, 72-hour vaporetto tickets, shopping, restaurants and hotels.

CHORUS (tel: 041-275 0462; www.chorusvenezia.org) offers a discount pass (€9) valid for entrance to 15 churches, which may be purchased at participating churches.

Flights: in high season from the UK from £100–250 return depending on the airline, date and time of travel.

Hotel: in high season, double room with breakfast, inclusive of tax: deluxe, €400 plus; expensive, €250–400; moderate, €130–250; inexpensive, under €130.

Food: sandwiches from €1.30; meal at an inexpensive restaurant €25–30; at a moderate restaurant €40–50; pizza €7–12.
Drinks: beer €3–5; glass of house wine €2–5.
Museums and attractions: €2–10. A museum pass for all civic museums costs €18.
Entertainment: Casino €10 admission. A concert in a main church costs from €25–60. La Fenice opera tickets from €80.
Gondolas: The official daytime rate is €80 for 40 minutes (up to six people), then €40 for each subsequent 20 minutes. The evening rate (from 8pm–8am) is €100. Expect to pay more – gondoliers rarely respect the official rates. Serenaded gondola tours (40 min) are €35 per person.

C

CLIMATE

Winters are cold, summers are hot, and the rest of the year is somewhere in between. The winds off the Adriatic and occasional flooding mean that Venice can be damp and chilly, although very atmospheric, between November and March. June, July and August can be stifling – air-conditioning is essential for a good night's rest at this time of year.

		J	F	M	A	M	J	J	A	S	O	N	D
Max	°F	42	46	54	63	71	77	83	83	79	65	54	46
	°C	6	8	12	17	22	25	28	28	26	18	12	8
Min	°F	34	34	41	51	57	64	68	66	62	52	43	37
	°C	1	1	5	10	14	18	20	19	17	11	6	3

CLOTHING

A pair of comfortable walking shoes is essential – despite Venice's excellent canal transport network, if you want to sightsee, you'll probably spend most of your time on foot. Even in summer, pack a light jacket for breezy evening *vaporetto* rides. For winter trips, take lots of layers, including a warm coat. Some of the better hotels loan out knee boots in case of flooding and street vendors sell disposable above-the-knee plastic boots.

When visiting churches you won't be allowed in if your back and shoulders are uncovered or if your shorts go above the knee. Venice is generally an informal city, but stylish dress is appropriate at its smarter restaurants.

CRIME AND SAFETY (See also EMERGENCIES and POLICE)

Although Venice is one of the safest cities in Italy, pickpockets and purse-snatchers are not uncommon. Be careful on crowded public transport, especially when getting on and off the *vaporetti*, at the railway station, in the crush around San Marco and in deserted streets.

Make photocopies of your airline tickets, driving licence, passport, and other vital documents to facilitate reporting any theft and obtaining replacements. Report thefts to the police, so that you have a statement to file with your insurance claim.

I want to report a theft	**Voglio denunciare un furto**

D

DRIVING

Venice is a **traffic-free zone**, and the closest you can get to the centre in a car is Piazzale Roma, where there are multi-storey car parks. There is also a huge multi-level car park on the 'car-park' island of Tronchetto, the terminal for the car ferry to the Lido, where driving is allowed. There are also two car parks on the mainland at Mestre San Giuliano and Fusina, both of which have easy access to Venice by bus.

E

ELECTRICITY

The current is 220V, AC; sockets take two-pin round-pronged plugs.

I'd like an adaptor/a battery	**Vorrei una presa complementare/una batteria**

EMBASSIES AND CONSULATES *(Ambasciate, Consolati)*

The nearest embassies and consulates to Venice are as follows:

Australia: Via Antonio Bosio 5, Rome; tel: 06-852 721, www.italy.embassy.gov.au.

Canada: Riviera Ruzzante 25, Padua; tel: 049-876 4833.

Ireland: Piazza di Campitelli 3, Rome; tel: 06-697 9121, www.ambasciata-irlanda.it.

New Zealand: Via Clitunno 44, Rome, tel: 06-853 7501; www.nzembassy.com/italy.

South Africa: Santa Croce 466G, Piazzale Roma, Venice; tel: 041-524 1599, www.sudafrica.it.

UK: Piazzale Donatori di Sangue 2, Mestre; tel: 041-505 5990; www.ukve.it.

US: Via Principe Amedeo 2/10, Milan; tel: 02-290 351; http://milan.usconsulate.gov.

EMERGENCIES

In case of an emergency, telephone:

Police **112**	Carabinieri (for urgent police action) **113**
Fire **115**	Ambulance **118**

Help (police)!	**Polizia!**	Fire!	**Incendio!**
Stop! Thief!	**Al ladro!**	Stop!	**Stop!**

G

GAY AND LESBIAN TRAVELLERS

A conservative city with an average age of 45, Venice has very few gay and lesbian venues. Padova, 32km (20 miles) away and easily reached by train or bus, is a better bet. At Mestre, near Venice, Porto de Mar at Via delle Macchine 41–43 (www.portodemar.com) is a lively gay bar with themed nights.

GETTING THERE

By air. Companies flying to Venice from the UK include British Airways (tel: 0870-551 1155; www.ba.com), who operate flights from Gatwick, bmi (tel: 0870-607 0555; www.flybmi.com), who fly from Heathrow, and easyJet (tel: 0905-821 0905; www.easyjet.com), who fly from Gatwick, Bristol and East Midlands airports.

Ryanair (tel: 0871-246 0000; www.ryanair.com) run flights from Stansted to Treviso airport (20 miles from Venice). There are also summer charters on offer to travellers from Gatwick, Manchester, Birmingham and other regional airports. Aer Lingus (tel: 0870 876 5000; www.flyaerlingus.com) operates services from Dublin to Venice.

From the US there are direct seasonal flights to Venice from New York (Delta Airlines; www.delta.com) and from Philadelphia (US Airways; www.usairways.com). Other flights go via Rome or Milan. From Australia and New Zealand, flights are generally to Rome, with onward connections.

Within Italy there are direct flights to Venice from Milan, Naples, Rome and Palermo.

By train. Venice is very well connected by train. Its main station is Stazione Venezia–Santa Lucia. Fastest travel time is 2 hours 30 minutes to Milan, 2 hours 40 minutes to Florence and 4 hours to Rome. For timetables and bookings visit www.trenitalia.it.

InterRail passes (www.raileurope.co.uk) are valid in Italy, as is the **Eurailpass** for non-European residents (buy it before you leave home). However, unless you are travelling very extensively it will probably work out cheaper to buy rail tickets as you go.

By bus. Buses from within Italy arrive in Venice at Piazzale Roma.

By car. If you travel by car, you will need a current driving licence (with an Italian translation unless it is the standard EU licence) and valid insurance (green card). The Channel Tunnel and Cross-Channel car ferries link the UK with France, Belgium and Holland. The travelling distance from the UK to Venice is 1,350km (844 miles) taking 13–14 hours, virtually all on motorway. Visit www.viamichelin.com for route planning and details of cost of petrol and road tolls. Having a car won't help you once you reach Venice, however, as they are not allowed in the centre and must be left in a car park *(see page 117)*.

GUIDES AND TOURS

The tourist office *(see pages 127–8)* can supply you with a list of qualified tour guides if you want a personal tour of a particular site or on a specialist aspect of Venice. All year round there are standard tours (book through hotels and travel agencies), including a two-hour **walking tour** of San Marco, taking in the Basilica and the Palazzo Ducale; a two-hour **walking and gondola tour** covering the Frari and the Grand Canal; a one-hour evening **gondola serenade** tour; and a three-hour **islands tour**. It costs more to go on an organised tour than to visit the same places independently.

A **cruise** along the Brenta Canal to Padua, aboard the 200-seater *Burchiello* motorboat, makes an interesting day out (although expensive at €71, plus €26 extra for lunch); book through local travel agencies and hotels. The return journey to Venice is by coach.

Free tours are given of the Basilica in summer, while 'Secret Tours' (*Itinerari Segreti*; charge) show you the ins and outs of life at the Palazzo Ducale *(see page 38)*.

Evening lectures on the **art and history** of Venice are held during the summer months. Ask at the tourist office for details. For more information on guided tours consult www.tours-italy.com.

H

HEALTH AND MEDICAL CARE

EU residents should obtain an EHIC (European Health Insurance Card), available from post offices or online at www.ehic.org.uk, which entitles them to emergency medical and hospital treatment.

Ask at your hotel if you need a doctor (or dentist) who speaks English. The US and British consulates *(see page 118)* have lists of English-speaking doctors. Many doctors at Venice's main hospital *(ospedale),* next to San Zanipolo church, speak English; for the casualty department *(pronto soccorso),* where medical emergencies are handled, tel: 041-529 4516.

Mosquitoes can be a nuisance in summer, so take along a small plug-in machine that burns a tablet emitting fumes that are noxious to them. Take cream with you to soothe bites.

Tap water is safe to drink, although locals prefer mineral water.
Pharmacies. Italian *farmacias* open during shopping hours and in turn for night and holiday service; the address of the nearest open pharmacy is posted on all pharmacy doors. You can also check the list in *Un Ospite di Venezia (see page 122)* or consult the local press.

I need a doctor/dentist	**Ho bisogno di un medico/dentista**
I've a pain here	**Ho un dolore qui**
a stomach ache	**il mal di stomaco**
a fever	**la febbre**

L

LANGUAGE

All Venetian hotels have staff who speak some English, as do most shops and restaurants. However, in some bars and cafés away from Piazza San Marco, you'll have the chance to practise your Italian.

Useful terms include: *piazza* (there is only one in Venice – San Marco); other squares are usually called *campo*, although a small square may be known as a *piazzetta*; the term *calle* is used to refer to streets, but a *salizzada* is a main street, and a covered passage is a *sottoportego*. A *ponte* is a bridge, a canal is a *rio*, and the paved walk-way along a major waterfront or *canale* is a *riva* or *fondamenta*.

Venetians have a strong dialect, and both Venetian and Italian names are used in street signs and on maps: San Giuliano is 'San Zulian' and Santi Giovanni e Paolo is 'San Zanipolo'.

In Italian the letter 'c' is pronounced 'ch' (as in church) when it is followed by 'e' or 'i,' while 'ch' is a hard sound, like the 'c' in cat.

LOST PROPERTY *(Oggetti Rinvenuti)*

The lost property office, *Ufficio Oggetti Rinvenuti*, is located at Ca' Loredan on Riva del Carbon, near the Rialto Bridge (tel: 041-274 8225; Mon–Fri 8.30am–12.30pm and Mon, Thur 2.30–4.30pm). If you lose something on a *vaporetto*, the lost property office (daily 9am–8pm) is in the ACTV building at Piazzale Roma. There are also lost property offices at the airport and railway station.

M

MAPS

Tourist information offices *(see pages 127–8)* sell the *Venezia e Isole* map and *Easyguide* accompanying booklet. This is useful for locat-ing sights and landing stages, but those who plan to stay in Venice any length of time should buy the Touring Club Italiano 1:5000 map.

MEDIA

Newspapers and magazines *(giornali, riviste)*. Venice's useful free listings magazine *Un Ospite di Venezia* (www.aguestinvenice.com) comes out fortnightly in season, monthly off season, but is only available in a few upmarket hotels. Look out also for *La Rivista di*

Venezia (Venice Magazine) in English and Italian, which comes with a useful 'What's On' booklet.

Radio and TV *(radio, televisione)*. The Italian state TV network, the RAI *(Radio Televisione Italiana)*, broadcasts three TV channels, which compete with a large number of independent ones. All programmes are in Italian; English-language imports are dubbed. The three state-owned radio stations, RAI-1, RAI-2 and RAI-3, offer classical and popular music, news, talk shows and sport.

Do you have English-language newspapers?	**Avete giornali in inglese?**

MONEY

Currency. Italy's monetary unit is the euro (abbreviated €), which is divided into 100 cents. Banknotes are available in denominations of 500, 200, 100, 50, 20, 10 and 5 euros. There are coins for 2 and 1 euros, and for 50, 20, 10, 5, 2 and 1 cents.

Currency exchange. The opening hours of currency exchange offices *(cambios)* are more convenient than those of banks but they charge higher rates of commission and exchange.

ATMs. Widespread throughout the city, these are the easiest means of accessing cash, however, some cards incur high transaction fees.

Traveller's cheques. Traveller's cheques are accepted in most places but are subject to high commission charges. You will usually get better value if you exchange them at a bank, though this can be a lengthy process and you will need to take your passport.

OPENING HOURS

Shops. Mon–Sat 9 or 10am–1pm, and 3 or 4pm–7pm. Some shops are open all day and even on Sundays, particularly in peak season.

Banks: Mon–Fri 8.30am–1.30pm, 2.35–3.35pm.

Bars and restaurants: Some café-bars open for breakfast, but others do not open until around noon; the vast majority shut at around 10.30 or 11pm. Most restaurants close for at least one day per week, and some close for parts of August, January and February.

Churches. The 15 CHORUS churches *(see page 115)* are open Mon–Sat 10am–5pm. Other churches are normally open Mon–Sat 8am–noon and 3 or 4pm–6 or 7pm. Sunday openings vary, some are only open for morning services.

Museums and galleries. Some close one day a week, usually Monday or Tuesday, and are otherwise open from 9 or 10am until 6pm.

P

POLICE *(Polizia, Carabinieri. See also EMERGENCIES)*

Venice's police are efficient and courteous. The emergency police telephone numbers are **112** and **113**, which will put you through to a switchboard and someone who speaks your language. The *vigili urbani* or municipal police enforce local laws and wear blue uniforms in winter, white in summer. The *carabinieri*, with a red stripe on their trousers, are the armed military police, responsible for public law and order and the *polizia di stato*, in blue uniforms, are the state police.

The main police station or Questura is at Santa Croce 500, Piazzale Roma, tel 041 2715511.

Where's the nearest police station?	**Dov'è il più vicino posto di polizia?**

POST OFFICES *(Posta, Ufficio Postale)*

The main office (Mon–Sat 8.30am–6.30pm) is inside the Fondachi dei Tedeschi at the Rialto. The lobby of the main office can be used 24 hours a day for express and registered letters.

Postage stamps *(francobolli)* are also sold at tobacconists *(tabacchi)*, marked by a distinctive 'T' sign.

I'd like a stamp for this letter/postcard	**Desidero un francobollo per questa lettera/cartolina**

PUBLIC HOLIDAYS *(Giorni Festivi)*

Banks, government offices and most shops and museums close on public holidays. When a major holiday falls on a Thursday or a Tuesday, Italians may make a *ponte* (bridge) to the weekend, meaning that Friday or Monday is taken, too. The most important are:

1 January	**Capodanno**	New Year's Day
6 January	**Epifania**	Epiphany
25 April	**Festa della Liberazione**	Liberation Day
1 May	**Festa del Lavoro**	Labour Day
25 August	**Ferragosto**	Assumption Day
1 November	**Ognissanti**	All Saints' Day
8 December	**Immacolata Concezione**	Immaculate Conception
25 December	**Natale**	Christmas Day
26 December	**Santo Stefano**	St Stephen's Day
Movable date	**Lunedì di Pasqua**	Easter Monday

The **Festa della Salute** on 21 November is a special Venetian holiday, when many shops close.

R

RELIGION

Although predominantly Roman Catholic, Venice has congregations of all the major religions. Check in *Un Ospite di Venezia (see page 122)* or ask at your hotel or the local tourist office for details.

T

TELEPHONES *(Telefoni)*

The country code for Italy is 39, and the area code for the city of Venice is 041. Note that whether phoning from abroad or within the city you must always dial the '041' prefix.

Telecom Italia public phones, which can be used for long distance and international calls, can be found all over the city. For these you need coins or phone cards *(schede telefoniche)* which are sold in tobacconists and post offices in denominations from €5. You must insert a coin or a card to access a dial tone even when making a toll-free call. Pre-paid international phone cards are better value for phoning abroad – for these you dial a toll-free number found on the back of the card. To make an international call, dial 00, followed by the country code and finally the individual number.

EU mobile phones can be used in Italy, but check compatibility before you leave. Charges for using a UK-based mobile to make and receive calls and texts abroad are high. If you are in Italy for some time it's worth purchasing an Italian 'pay as you go' SIM card for the length of your stay.

TIME ZONES

Italy follows Central European Time (GMT+1) and from late March to late September clocks are put one hour ahead (GMT+2). The following chart indicates time differences during the summer:

New York	London	**Venice**	Jo'burg	Sydney	Auckland
6am	11am	**noon**	noon	8pm	10pm

TIPPING

Tipping is not taken for granted in Italy, though a bit extra will always be appreciated. A service charge of around 10 or 12 percent is often added to restaurant bills; otherwise a 10 percent tip is ample. It is normal practice to tip porters (€1–2 per bag), bellboys, maids (€1–2 per day), tour guides and the elderly gondolier posted at the landing station who helps you into and out of your craft.

| Keep the change. | **Tenga il resto.** |

TOILETS *(Toilette, Gabinetti)*

There are public toilets (usually of a reasonable standard but with a charge) in the airport, railway station, car parks and in some main squares in the city. *Signori* means men; *signore* means women.

| Where are the toilets? | **Dove sono i gabinetti?** |

TOURIST INFORMATION

The **Italian National Tourist Board** (ENIT; www.enit.it) has several offices abroad:

Australia: Level 26, 44 Market Street, Sydney; tel: 02-9262 1666.
Canada: 175 Bloor Street East, Suite 907, South Tower, Toronto, Ontario M4W 3R8; tel: 416-925 4882; www.italiantourism.com.
UK/Ireland: 1 Princes Street, London W1B 2AY; tel: 020-7408 1254; www.enit.it.
US: www.italiantourism.com. **Chicago:** 500 N Michigan Avenue, Suite 506 Chicago, IL 60611; tel: 312-644 0996. **Los Angeles:** 12400 Wilshire Boulevard, Suite 550, Los Angeles CA 90025; tel: 310-820 1898. **New York:** 630 Fifth Avenue, Suite 1565, New York, NY 10111; tel: 212-245 5618.

The main tourist office in Venice (daily 10am–6pm; www.turismovenezia.it) is in the **Venice Pavilion** beside the Giardinetti Reali (public gardens). There is a smaller office on the western corner of **Piazza San Marco** opposite the Correr Museum entrance (tel: 041-529 8711; daily 9am–3.30pm). There are also tourist offices at the **railway station** (daily 8am–6.30pm) and **airport** (daily 9.30am–7.30pm).

TRANSPORT

Waterbuses (*vaporetti*). The only public transport in Venice is water-borne, and an efficient *vaporetto* will take you to within a short walk of anywhere you want to go. Venice is so compact, however, that for short journeys, it is often quicker (and cheaper) to walk. *Vaporetti* routes run along the Grand Canal, round the north and south shores of the city and to the minor islands and Lido. They run regularly throughout the day and provide a wonderful perspective on the city. A schedule for all *vaporetti* lines may be obtained from the ACTV office at Piazzale Roma, tel: 041-2424; www.actv.it.

Tickets can be purchased at most landing stages, any shop displaying an ACTV sign or once on board. A single ticket costs €6.50. Validate your ticket by stamping it at the machine on the landing stage; it is then valid for 90 minutes. Travel cards are a good investment if you plan to make several journeys a day: a 24-hour ticket costs €18, 48 hours €28 and 72 hours €33.

The main services used by tourists are: No. 1 (*accelerato*), which stops at every landing stage along the Grand Canal; No. 2 (*diretto*), providing a faster service down the Grand Canal as part of its circular San Marco, Giudecca Canal, Piazzale Roma route. For the island of Murano take Nos 41, 42, LN (Laguna Nord) or in summer No. 5. The LN, which departs from Fondamente Nuove, continues to Burano and Line T connects Burano with Torcello.

When's the next vaporetto for…?	**A che ore parte il prossimo vaporetto per…?**
What's the fare to…?	**Quanto costa il biglietto per…?**
I want a ticket to…	**Vorrei un biglietto per…**

Traghetti. The *traghetto* (gondola ferry) service operates at various points across the Grand Canal. It is customary (but not obligatory) to stand while crossing. The cost of using the *traghetto* is €0.50.

Water taxis. If you need a door-to-door service (or you want to avoid the crowds), ask your hotel to call a *motoscafo* or tel: 041-522 2303. Although fast, they are extremely expensive.

TRAVELLERS WITH DISABILITIES

Although the narrow alleys and numerous stepped bridges make the city tricky for disabled travellers there are ways and means of getting around and seeing at least some of the major sights. The larger *vaporetti* (such as numbers 1 and 2) have access for wheelchairs, but the slimmer *motoscafi* should be avoided. Any of the tourist offices can lend a key to operate the few wheelchair lifts for bridges, which are mainly in San Marco. Many of the other bridges now have wheelchair ramps.

If you understand Italian, **Informahandicap** has a useful website at www.comune.venezia.it/informahandicap and a branch at Ca'-Farsetti, Riva del Carbon, San Marco 4136, tel: 041-274 8144.

Accessible attractions (note, however, that no differentiation is made between full and partial access) include the Basilica di San Marco, Palazzo Ducale, Ca' Rezzonico, the churches of the Frari, La Salute, San Zanipolo and San Giorgio Maggiore, Museo Correr and some other museums.

V

VISAS AND ENTRY REQUIREMENTS

Citizens of EU countries need only a valid passport or identity card to enter Italy for stays of up to 90 days. Citizens of Australia, Canada, New Zealand and the US require only a valid passport; South Africans require a passport plus a visa, available from Italian consulates in South Africa.

Customs. Free exchange of non-duty-free goods for personal use is allowed between countries within the EU.

W

WEBSITES AND INTERNET ACCESS

The following are good places to research your trip to Venice:

www.turismovenezia.it – local tourist board website

www.meetingvenice.it – regional tourist board website

www.aguestinvenice.com – online version of the tourist magazine, packed with practical information

www.comune.venezia.it – city council's site, with many useful links

www.veneziasi.it – hotel booking website

www.veniceonline.it – lively site covering events, exhibitions, where to sleep and eat.

www.actv.it – waterbus maps and timetables

Internet access. Many hotels have Wifi access, either included in the room rate or charged by the hour. The website, www.venetian navigator.com, has a map showing Wifi hotspots in the city.

A passport is normally required for use of internet cafés. Close to Piazza San Marco, the Libreria Mondadori bookshop at San Marco 1345 has three internet points and long opening hours. Venetian Navigator has internet points both at Calle Caselleria, Castello 5300 and Calle Stagneri, San Marco 523.

Y

YOUTH HOSTELS *(Ostelli della Gioventù)*

Venice's only official hostel is the beautifully located HI (Hostelling International) hostel on the waterfront of Giudecca: Ostello Venezia (Fondamenta delle Zitelle, Giudecca 86; tel: 041-523 8211; www. ostellionline.org). Bed and breakfast costs €21–26 per person. Booking is essential in summer.

Recommended Hotels

The following is a just a selection of the many hotels in the city, organised by area. In general, the closer to San Marco, the more expensive a hotel will be. If you're looking for something slightly more economical, try across the Grand Canal in Dorsoduro or the less chic area around the Lista di Spagna near the railway station in Cannaregio. San Polo and Santa Croce, away from the main tourist haunts, offer better value than San Marco and are within walking distance of the main sights. The most luxurious hotels are mainly on the Grand Canal or on the Riva degli Schiavoni waterfront in Castello, close to San Marco.

The ranges below indicate the price of a double room with bath or shower per night, including breakfast and tax, during high season. The nearest vaporetto stop to a hotel is given at the end of each listing.

€€€€	€400 and above
€€€	€250–400
€€	€180–250
€	€180 and under

SAN MARCO

Ai Do Mori € *Calle Larga, San Marco 658, tel: 041-520 4817, fax: 041-520 5328, www.hotelaidomori.com.* Climb three flights to get to this tidy 11-roomed hotel just steps from the Basilica. It also has a nearby annexe with recently renewed rooms. In the main hotel, rooms on the upper floors have views of the domes of San Marco; the attic-level 'Painter's Room' (reserve months ahead) has a private deck and great vista. Excellent staff. No breakfast. ACTV: San Zaccaria.

Bel Sito & Berlino €–€€ *Campo Santa Maria del Giglio, San Marco 2517, tel: 041-522 3365, fax: 041-520 4083, www.hotelbel sito.info.* This friendly hotel, in a great location between Piazza San Marco and Accademia Bridge, has 34 bedrooms furnished in pleasant, traditional style. Rooms at the front overlook a lavish Baroque church; the ones at the rear of the hotel are quieter. Wheelchair access. ACTV: Santa Maria del Giglio.

Flora €€ *Calle della Pergola, off Calle Larga XXII Marzo, San Marco 2283/A, tel: 041-520 5844, fax: 041-522 8217, www.hotel flora.it.* Family-run Flora is in a great location and has 44 traditionally decorated rooms which vary in size. It has attractive public areas, a secluded little garden and wheelchair access. ACTV: Vallaresso.

Gritti Palace €€€€ *Campo Santa Maria del Giglio, San Marco 2467, tel: 041-794 611, fax: 041-520 0942, www.starwood.com.* In a 15th-century doge's palace overlooking the Grand Canal, the Gritti Palace offers the last word in traditional grandeur and personal attention. The 91 rooms are beautiful – many have hand-painted 18th-century decor. Wheelchair access. ACTV: Santa Maria del Giglio.

Kette €€–€€€ *Piscina San Moisè, San Marco 2053, tel: 041-520 7766, fax: 041-522 8964, www.hotelkette.com.* Located in a beautifully renovated old house with polished wood and warm mellow furnishings extending to the bedrooms, this mid-sized hotel is particularly popular with tour groups. Just a short hop from Piazza San Marco. Wheelchair access. ACTV: Vallaresso.

La Fenice et des Artistes €€–€€€ *Campiello della Fenice, San Marco 1936, tel: 041-523 2333, fax: 041-520 3721, www.fenice hotels.com.* This atmospheric 65-roomed hotel located next to the site of the Fenice opera house *(see pages 89–90)* tends to attract visitors interested in the arts; it's popular with musicians too. In one wing, rooms are decorated traditionally, while in the other they are modern and a little bland; most are air-conditioned. Amenities include terraces and a garden. ACTV: Santa Maria del Giglio.

Locanda Art Deco € *Calle delle Botteghe, San Marco 2966, tel: 041-277 058, fax: 041-270 2891, www.locandaartdeco.com.* Charming little bed and breakfast in a quiet street off Campo Santo Stefano. Guest rooms are individually furnished, with art deco touches. Minimum 3 night stays at weekends. ACTV: Sant'Angelo.

Luna Baglioni €€€€ *Calle Vallaresso, San Marco 1243, tel: 041-528 9840, fax: 041-528 7160, www.baglionihotels.com.* This large, heavily modernised hotel beside Piazza San Marco has five-star aspirations and an historic pedigree. The public rooms are splendid, but only a quarter of the traditionally furnished bedrooms have good views. Wheelchair access. ACTV: Vallaresso.

Novecento €€ *Calle del Dose, San Marco 2683, tel: 041-241 3765, fax: 041-521 2145, www.locandanovecento.it.* A warm and welcoming little hotel located a few minutes' walk from Piazza San Marco. Opened in 2001, it is owned by the Romanelli family, as is the Flora *(see opposite)*, but is very different in style. Decor is an imaginative blend of Moroccan, Turkish and oriental styles. There are just nine rooms, all individually furnished. Good buffet breakfasts are served in the pretty little courtyard in summer. ACTV: Santa Maria del Giglio.

San Samuele € *Salizzada San Samuele, San Marco 3358, tel/fax: 041-520 5165, www.albergosansamuele.it.* Ten simple rooms, both with and without private bathrooms, in a bright friendly place on a street dominated by trendy galleries. ACTV: San Samuele.

Saturnia & International €€€–€€€€ *Via XXII Marzo, San Marco 2398, tel: 041-520 8377, fax: 041-520 7131, www.hotelsaturnia.it.* Built around a 14th-century doge's palace, this large hotel has been run by the same family since 1908. The rooms in the old part are more sumptuous than those in the new section. Wheelchair access. ACTV: Vallaresso.

Violino d'Oro €€–€€€ *Campiello Barozzi, San Marco 2091, tel: 041-277 0841, fax: 041-277 1001, www.violinodoro.com.* Just steps from San Marco, this hotel offers 26 tastefully designed rooms. Wheelchair access. ACTV: Vallaresso.

Westin Europa & Regina €€€€ *San Marco 2159, tel: 041-240 0001, www.starwoodhotels.com/westin.* This large, renowned Grand Canal hotel has spectacular terrace views over Santa Maria della Salute. There is an excellent canalfront restaurant and beach and recreation facilities at the Lido. Wheelchair access. ACTV: Vallaresso.

CASTELLO

Bisanzio €€–€€€ *Calle della Pietà, Castello 3651, tel: 041-520 3100, fax: 041-520 4114, www.hotelbisanzio.com.* In a peaceful spot just off the Riva degli Schiavoni, the recently renovated Bisanzio has 47 simply furnished traditional rooms, a courtyard and terraces. ACTV: San Zaccaria.

Campiello €€ *Calle del Vin, San Zaccaria, Castello, 4647, tel: 041-520 5764, fax: 041-520 5798, www.hcampiello.it.* A well-run, family-owned hotel located just off the Riva degli Schiavoni with cosy public areas and 16 traditional rooms. ACTV: San Zaccaria.

Casa Verardo €€–€€€ *Camp SS Filippo e Giacomo, Castello 4765, tel: 041-528 6138, fax: 041-523 2765, www.casaverardo.it.* This intimate, family-run hotel in a small, renovated 16th-century palace is extremely central (around 200m/yds from Piazza San Marco), despite being tucked away and quite tricky to find. Traditional, spacious rooms. ACTV: San Zaccaria.

Castello € *Calle della Sacrestia, off Campo Santi Filippo e Giacomo, Castello 4365, tel: 041-523 0217, fax: 041-521 1023, www.hotelcastello.it.* The Castello is a small, cosy hotel next to a lively square. The 26 rooms are decorated in classic Venetian style and equipped with modern amenities. ACTV: San Zaccaria.

Colombina €€€ *Calle del Remedio, Castello 4416, tel: 041-277 0525, fax: 041-277 6044, www.hotelcolombina.com.* This lovely hotel is in a canalside *palazzo* overlooking the Bridge of Sighs. It has 33 tastefully decorated rooms and a 3-star annexe behind the hotel. Two quaint top-floor rooms have roof decks with wonderful views of San Marco. Wheelchair access. ACTV: San Zaccaria.

Danieli €€€€ *Riva degli Schiavoni, Castello 4196, tel: 041-522 6480, fax: 041-520 0208, www.starwoodhotels.com.* The most dramatic of Venice's luxury hotels, situated beside the Palazzo Ducale, the Danieli has sumptuous neo-Gothic public areas set around a balconied staircase, a rooftop restaurant with sweeping vistas, and suites furnished with antiques. Note that the majority of doubles are in newer wings. The hotel has private beach facilities at the Lido. Wheelchair access. ACTV: San Zaccaria.

Gabrielli Sandwirth €€€–€€€€ *Riva degli Schiavoni, Castello 4110, tel: 041-523 1580, fax: 041-520 9455, www.hotelgabrielli.it.* Set in a Gothic palace, with great vistas from its rooftop sun terrace, this large hotel has rooms with pleasant, traditional decor and 1960s-style public areas, which are rather in need of updating. In summer meals are served in a pretty courtyard. Also has a private garden. ACTV: San Zaccaria or Arsenale.

La Residenza €–€€ *Campo Bandiera e Moro, Castello 3608, tel: 041-528 5315, fax: 041-523 8859, www.venicelaresidenza.com.* An atmospheric 15th-century palace with unusual public areas. Set on a pleasant square, the hotel offers just 15 simple but adequate bedrooms – book ahead to ensure one of the best ones. ACTV: San Zaccaria or Arsenale.

Metropole €€€–€€€€ *Riva degli Schiavoni, Castello 4149, tel: 041-520 5044, fax: 041-522 3679, www.hotelmetropole.com.* This restored early-19th-century building facing the lagoon has 67 tasteful rooms, peppered with antiques. Fantastic service and a Michelin-starred restaurant. ACTV: San Zaccaria.

Savoia & Jolanda €€€–€€€€ *Riva degli Schiavoni, Castello 4187, tel: 041-520 6644, fax: 041-520 7494, www.hotelsavoiajolanda. com.* This grand-looking establishment has many rooms with balconies opening on to the lagoon. Bedrooms have been decorated in traditional style; there's an annex with cheaper, simpler rooms. Wheelchair access. ACTV: San Zaccaria.

Vivaldi €€€–€€€€ *Riva degli Schiavoni, Castello 4152-3, tel: 041-277 0477, fax: 041-277 0489, www.locandavivaldi.it.* The Vivaldi is notable for its opulent Baroque-style decor. Its 25 well-appointed rooms are tasteful but varied in appeal: some are spacious, with views of the lagoon, while others are rather small. Wheelchair access. ACTV: San Zaccaria.

DORSODURO

Agli Alboretti €€ *Rio Terrà Antonio Foscarini, Dorsoduro 884, tel: 041-523 0058, fax: 041-521 0158, www.aglialboretti.com.* Lovely family-run hotel with nautical-themed decor and quaint rooms. ACTV: Accademia or Zattere.

American Dinesen €€€ *San Vio, Dorsoduro 628, tel: 041-520 4733, fax: 041-520 4048, www.hotelamerican.it.* All the rooms of this small, well-run hotel are furnished in tasteful, traditional Venetian style. Pretty canalside setting. ACTV: Accademia.

Ca' della Corte €€ *Corte Surian, Dorsoduro 3560, tel: 041-715 877, fax: 041-722 345, www.cadellacorte.com.* An inviting B&B hidden away in a northern corner of Dorsoduro, but only 3 minutes from Piazza Roma. Staff are welcoming, guest rooms elegantly and thoughtfully furnished. Apartments are also available. ACTV: Piazzale Roma.

Ca' Pisani €€€ *Rio Terrà Antonio Foscarini, Dorsoduro 979a, tel: 041-240 1411, fax: 041-277 1061, www.capisanihotel.it.* Venice's first designer hotel, converted from a 16th-century palazzo close to the Accademia. Minimalist decor with stylish Art Deco furnishings and features. Bedrooms come with internet connection and state-of-the-art bathrooms. Facilities include a roof-top terrace and the Rivista bar and restaurant offering Venetian fare with a modern twist. ACTV: Accademia.

Messner € *Salute, Dorsoduro 216, tel: 041-522 7443, fax: 041-522 7266, www.hotelmessner.it.* Messner is a small, well-run hotel on a quiet street close to the church of Santa Maria della Salute. It has a restaurant, small, adequately comfortable bedrooms, both in the main house and annexe, and a breakfast terrace. It is one of the more affordable of Venice's hotels, popular with a younger clientele and student groups. ACTV: Salute.

Pensione Accademia Villa Maravege €€–€€€ *Fondamenta Bollani, Dorsoduro 1058, tel: 041-521 0188, fax: 041-523 9152, www.pensioneaccademia.it.* A small, traditional and gorgeous hotel in a

17th-century villa (the setting for the film *Summertime*, starring Katharine Hepburn), with delightful gardens. Excellent location close to the Accademia. Popular, so book well ahead. ACTV: Accademia.

SAN POLO AND SANTA CROCE

Antica Locanda Sturion €€–€€€ *Calle del Sturion, San Polo 679, tel: 041-523 6243, fax: 041-522 8378, www.locandasturion.com.* The Locanda Sturion is on the top floor of an historic building near the Rialto markets, with its breakfast room overlooking the Grand Canal. Elaborate baroque-style decor. 11 rooms. ACTV: Rialto.

Ca' Malcanton €–€€ *Salizada San Pantalon, Santa Croce 49, tel: 041-710 931, www.venice4you.co.uk.* An upmarket, English-owned B&B in a cleverly reconstructed Venetian palazzo. Guests are encouraged to use the beautiful main salon for reading, relaxing (and watching satellite TV). This opens out onto a canalside garden where breakfasts are taken in summer. The five comfortable guest rooms all have stylish bathrooms. ACTV: Piazzale Roma.

San Cassiano (Ca' Favretto) €€€ *Calle della Rosa, Santa Croce 2232, tel: 041-524 1768, fax: 041-721 033, www.sancassiano.it.* In an atmospheric 14th-century palace slightly off the beaten track. The 35 rooms are well equipped; the most popular ones are facing the Ca' d'Oro over the Grand Canal. Wheelchair access. ACTV: San Stae.

CANNAREGIO

Bernardi–Semanzato € *Santi Apostoli, Cannaregio 4363, tel: 041-522 7257, fax: 041-522 2424, www.hotelbernardi.com.* This hotel, situated north of the Rialto, has helpful staff and 14 plain but modern rooms, 12 with private bathrooms. ACTV: Ca' d'Oro.

Dei Dogi €€€–€€€€ *Fondamenta Madonna dell'Orto, Cannaregio 3500, tel: 041-220 8111, fax: 041-722 278, www.boscolohotels.it.* The 18th-century Palazzo Rizzo Patarol, previously the seat of the French and Savoy embassies, has been converted into a 5-star hotel. Advantages over the more central hotels are the extensive gardens leading down to the lagoon, a peaceful setting in the pretty Madonna dell' Orto neighbour and reasonable rates for 5 star luxury. Hourly water shuttle to the centre. ACTV: Orto.

Giorgione €€–€€€ *SS Apostoli, Cannaregio 4587, tel: 041-522 5810, fax: 041-523 9092, www.hotelgiorgione.com.* This is a delightful hotel with 70 comfortable, renovated rooms. The fact that there are no water views, and that it is in Cannaregio, make it comparatively well priced for its class. The nicest rooms are the doubles with tiny private roof decks and the terrace suites. ACTV: Ca' d'Oro.

Locanda Leon Bianco €–€€ *Corte del Leon Bianco, Cannaregio 5629, tel: 041-523 3572, fax: 041-241 6392, www.leonbianco.it.* This seven-roomed hotel is entered through an unprepossessing courtyard and foyer that were once part of a Grand Canal palace. Upstairs, the traditional rooms are very comfortable – three spacious rooms with spectacular canal vistas offer excellent value. ACTV: Ca' d'Oro.

Palazzo Abadessa €€€ *Calle Priuli, Cannaregio 4011, tel: 041-241 3784, fax: 041-521 2236, www.abadessa.com.* This magnificent Venetian palazzo was converted into an exclusive hotel five years ago. Sumptuous rooms are furnished with original paintings and frescoes, huge Murano chandeliers, and silk-lined walls. Maria Luisa Rossi who owns the palazzo is a charming host who makes you feel at home in this romantic residence. ACTV: Ca' d'Oro.

GIUDECCA

Hilton Molino Stucky €€€€ *Giudecca 753, tel/fax: 041-522 1267, www.molinostuckyhilton.com.* This 19th-century flour mill on the Giudecca waterfront was recently converted into a 380-room 5-star hotel and Venice's largest Hotel Congress Centre. The rooftop outdoor swimming pool has grand views of Venice. Wheelchair access. ACTV: Polanca.

Hotel Cipriani €€€€ *Giudecca 10, tel: 041-520 7744, fax: 041-520 3930, www.hotelcipriani.com.* Arguably Venice's most luxurious hotel, the Cipriani consists of modern buildings set in a lovely

garden with a swimming pool, and its 98 rooms have every ameni-
ty – those in the 15th-century Palazzo Vendramin annexe even come
with a butler. A hotel launch shuttles guests to and from San Marco.
Wheelchair access. ACTV: Zitelle.

THE LIDO

Grand Hotel Des Bains €€€€ *Lungomare Marconi 17, tel: 041-
526 5921, fax: 041-526 0113, www.grandhoteldebainsvenezia.com.*
Forever associated with Visconti's *Death in Venice* (partly filmed
here) and Thomas Mann *(see page 86)*, this grand hotel with a large
garden, two tennis courts and a swimming pool is full of Belle
Epoque ambience. Faces its private beach on the Lido. Popular with
movie stars during the Film Festival. 195 rooms. Open Apr–Oct.

Rigel €€ *Via Enrico Dandolo 13, tel: 041-526 8810, fax: 041-276
0077, www.hotelrigel.it.* This friendly hotel, built in the 1960s, is
set in its own garden and situated close to the Piazzale Santa Maria
Elisabetta. Open Apr–Oct.

Westin Excelsior €€€€ *Lungomare Marconi 41, tel: 041-240
0001, www.starwoodhotels.com.* The Lido's only 5-star hotel, this
beachside Moorish-Gothic fantasy, constructed during the early
1900s, was originally billed as the most glamorous resort hotel
in the world. It offers 189 large, modern rooms, seven tennis
courts and a swimming pool. There's also a free launch service to
Venice. Probably a choice for business travellers or families rather
than those wanting the most romantic option. Open Apr–Oct.

SAN CLEMENTE

San Clemente Palace €€€–€€€€ *Isola di San Clemente 1, tel: 041-
244 5001, fax: 041-244 5800, www.sanclemente.thi-hotels.com.*
One of the cheaper 5-star Venetian hotels, the San Clemente Palace
is set on the small island of San Clemente in the southern lagoon.
A 10-minute shuttle service links it to San Marco. In the past San
Clemente has been a monastery island, military depot, cats' home
and lunatic asylum. Today it's a luxury award-winning resort hotel.

INDEX

Berlitz® pocket guide
Venice

Fifteenth Edition 2010
Reprinted 2012 (twice)

Written by Rob Ullian
Updated by Susie Boulton
Edited by Anna Tyler
Series Editor: Tom Stainer

Photography credits
All photography by Anna Mockford and Nick
Bonetti except: AKG 18, 20; Chris Coe 8, 9, 11,
12, 43, 59, 81, 88; Jon Davison 5TR; Glyn Genin
10, 29, 32, 42, 44, 51, 53, 54, 65, 67, 70, 76, 83,
96; istockphoto 1, 57, 87; Benjamin W.G. Legde
15; Mary Evans Picture Library 16; Ros Miller
28, 30, 84.

Cover picture: Sergio Pitamitz/Corbis

Every effort has been made to provide
accurate information in this publication,
but changes are inevitable. The publisher
cannot be responsible for any resulting
loss, inconvenience or injury.

Contact us
At Berlitz we strive to keep our guides as
accurate and up to date as possible, but if you
find anything that has changed, or if you have
any suggestions on ways to improve this guide,
then we would be delighted to hear from you.

Berlitz Publishing, PO Box 7910,
London SE1 1WE, England
email: berlitz@apaguide.co.uk
www.insightguides.com/berlitz

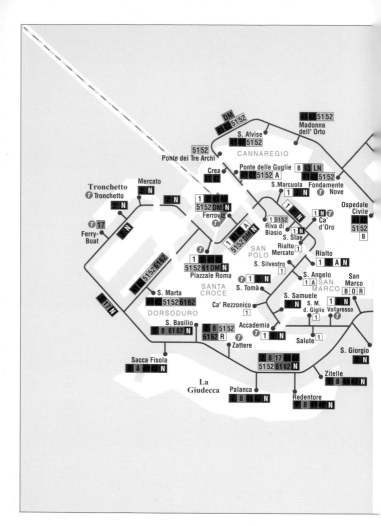

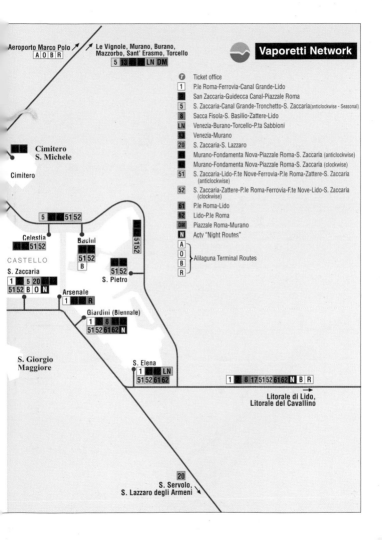